I have seen Paul Murphy in action. He writes of what he knows and practices. Paul shares lessons learned on the front lines in real-life engagement with church congregations. Biblically grounded with practical applications and engaging illustrations, anyone who wants to "up their game" in the arena of leadership—pastors, elders, laypeople alike—will benefit from reading and applying Paul's book.

Mark McCloskey, Professor of Ministry Leadership, Bethel Seminary, St. Paul, Minnesota

. . . .

I've had the opportunity to work alongside Paul Murphy at a number of churches. A gifted leader, Paul is passionate to see leaders and churches thrive. Anchored in a desire to see people experience genuine transformation, Paul's heart for leadership development is contagious. Each chapter is a wealth of wisdom with insightful questions that will help you dig deeper into your own growth as a leader. This book will be an essential part of my leadership toolbox and a resource I will turn to often. I'm thankful for Paul's impact on my life and trust this book will impact you in meaningful ways!

Jon Taylor, Campus Pastor, Eagle Brook Church, White Bear Lake, Minnesota

. . . .

I have worked with Paul firsthand and seen his passion for helping churches through leadership transitions. God has given him a unique calling and gifted him to love and lead in some of the most difficult situations. This book is a great summary of many of his experiences of leading in truth and grace. Paul's personal transparency and humility in regards to the challenges of leading like Jesus in a Christian organization are both encouraging and healing. If you are leading, or considering leading, this book will provide practical advice and inspiration to stay the course.

Cade M. Lambert, Superintendent, Des Moines Christian Schools, West Des Moines, Iowa

. . . .

What's it like on the inside being a pastor when things go south? Paul takes us there with great transparency, offering a whole lot of practical help along the way. I have seen this working up close in the lives and ministries of many leaders in the two-thirds underdeveloped world countries where Paul and I have teamed together training leaders.

Mark Wold, Reach Global, The Evangelical Free Church of America, Bloomington, Minnesota

. . . .

Exceedingly well-written. This is one of those "next to the bed" books. You can open any page and be both renewed and encouraged by Paul's God-inspired testimony.

Michael Morrison, Ph.D., Founder, University of Toyota, and Author, *The Other Side of the Card*

. . . .

Paul Murphy's long-term experience as a pastor in various churches, in which he had to navigate numerous challenging issues, prepared him extremely well for his present ministry of intentional interim pastorates that are designed to help churches in crisis or in transition emerge with health, strength, and vitality. The effectiveness of his dynamic, turn-around strategies speaks for itself: the churches he has worked with are healthy and flourishing. Paul has, to put it in a nutshell, "street cred!" What you have in your hands is a treasure trove of field-tested insights and strategies that will help failing churches turn around and will help healthy churches thrive even more!

Dr. Vic Copan, Chair of the Ministry Leadership Studies Department; Associate Professor of Biblical Studies at Palm Beach Atlantic University, West Palm Beach, Florida.

. . . .

I love the practical nature of the book. I truly felt the "firm hand in the middle of your back" as you walked through real life situations, stories, events, conflicts. _Leading Well_ is like a Physician's desk reference. When leading a group, pastoring a church, starting the process of setting direction – this book has the theory, the stories, and the practical ideas relevant to our task as Christian leaders. Great stuff, Paul!

Steve Spellman, Reach Global, The Evangelical Free Church of America, Brazil, and Haiti

. . . .

I found _Leading Well_ both encouraging and highly challenging. It helped explain the "weariness" I have seen in many leaders I have worked with over the years and have more recently felt in myself. This book clearly points out the "de-railers" that make ministries, churches, and leaders unhealthy and ineffective in leading people God-ward and gives practical challenging recommendations for personal and organizational turn-around.

Jim Kirkwood, Vice President, Global Center for Technology Creation, General Mills, Golden Valley, Minnesota

. . . .

Thank you for sharing your experiences, giving concrete advice and applications, and using God's Word as the foundation for your book. Most of all, for reminding me, that God does the work and that a servant leader's job is to move people God-ward, for His glory. I want to be a sailboat, not a rowboat! You are a great coach and friend.

Polly Wright, Major Gifts Officer, Feed My Starving Children, Coon Rapids, Minnesota

. . . .

Well done! Pastor Paul Murphy is a man for whom I hold a great deal of respect. I have watched him work as he came to our church on an Interim basis. I hope that you absorb the practical and biblical truth of this book and commit to action plans to address relational and leadership issues in your church, home, and business.

John Griffith, former Executive Vice President of Property Development, Target Corporation; now Head of Global Operations, American Refugee Committee

. . . .

I am a servant-led Christian business leader always seeking to teach by example. This book provides great insight to help any leader who seeks the best life for himself and others in an ever more challenging world. Such a vulnerable and humorous personal story that kept me interested and connected.

Lee Timmerman, President, Precision Press, a division of Taylor Corporation, Mankato, Minnesota

. . . .

There is a lot of practical knowledge and help within these pages for new pastors and seasoned pastors alike, as well as lay-leaders. *Leading Well* reminds pastors that our first calling is to be imitators of Jesus. Paul draws from years of church leadership experience to share how to foster harmony, clarity, purpose, and progress in your church. Having worked closely with Paul at my church, I can speak firsthand of the benefits of this biblical approach to leadership. His practical guidance and organizational techniques are invaluable. *Leading Well* reminds us that Jesus is the head of the church, and we serve the church best by imitating His example of care, relationship, stewardship, and sacrifice.

Gary Clemmer, Executive Administrative Pastor, Ecclesia, Hollywood, California

. . . .

LEADING WELL
GOD'S FINGERPRINTS UPON YOUR LIFE AND MINISTRY

PAUL J. MURPHY

WESTBOW
PRESS®
A DIVISION OF THOMAS NELSON
& ZONDERVAN

Unless otherwise indicated,
Scripture taken from:

THE HOLY BIBLE, NEW INTERNATIONAL VERSION,
Copyright © 1973, 1978, 1984 International Bible Society.
Used by Permission of Zondervan Bible Publishers.

THE MESSAGE: THE BIBLE IN CONTEMPORARY ENGLISH,
Copyright © 1993, 1994, 1995, 1996, 2000, 2001, 2002.
Used by permission of NavPress Publishing Group.

THE HOLY BIBLE, NEW LIVING TRANSLATION,
Copyright© 1996, 2004, 2007 by Tyndale House Foundation.
Used by permission of Tyndale House Publishers, Inc.
Carol Stream, Illinois 60188
All rights reserved. Used by permission.

WestBow Press books may be ordered through booksellers or by contacting:

WestBow Press
A Division of Thomas Nelson & Zondervan
1663 Liberty Drive
Bloomington, IN 47403
www.westbowpress.com
1 (866) 928-1240

ISBN: 978-1-5127-7310-1 (sc)
ISBN: 978-1-5127-7311-8 (hc)
ISBN: 978-1-5127-7309-5 (e)

Library of Congress Control Number: 2017900917

Print information available on the last page.

WestBow Press rev. date: 3/17/2017

To Liz, my wife for life, 39 years into the journey together.
Your loving honesty, acceptance, and support
have shaped me more than anyone else.

Acknowledgements

This book has been gestating for years out of my own faith life in the Lord and hands-on experience in Christian ministry. In addition to the Lord's fingerprints in my life, there are many other human fingerprints that have contributed to this book becoming a reality.

Special thanks to John Bloomquist, a faithful friend and brother, who gifted his expertise by devoting scores of hours to detailed editing of the manuscript. A number of friends invested time to read the draft version of this book, offering their compliments and constructive critiques. The end result is better than what I would have produced on my own.

A well-deserved thank you to the board members of Progress & Joy for their commitment, support, and counsel to me. A network of 350 prayer partners faithfully pray for me and the ministry the Lord has given to me, including the writing of this book. Their prayers repeatedly make the difference, and move the Kingdom ahead. Their partnership makes this ministry fruitful – from turning around churches, to the publishing of this book, and the training of leaders in the two-thirds world.

Thank you to the congregations with whom I have worked. Each has added to God's fingerprints upon my life and ministry.

Thank you to my own family for their encouragement, light-hearted joking, and affirmation of me. Particular thanks to Colleen Murphy for her artistic talents in creating the cover design for this book.

Finally, thank you to the many friends I have been blessed with along the way. Full-time Christian ministry is an unusual vocation, but it also has rare blessings – friends who are brothers and sisters in Christ, spread across the country and the world. As we often say in our own family, "We *have the privilege of knowing so many quality people all over the place.*"

Paul J. Murphy
February 2017
www.progressandjoy.net

PROGRESS & JOY
RENEWING CHURCHES, DEVELOPING LEADERS

Table of Contents

PURPOSE

God only needs leaders for one unchanging purpose. Without exception, the biblical evidence about leadership unfolds a consistent picture – God only appoints leaders for one, unchanging purpose.

Your life as a leader is a message and a ministry. The good news gospel of Jesus is life-changing. It will change us, and change how we treat others. How Jesus treats us is to become how we treat people. The Vertical is to become the Horizontal.

What is a healthy, productive church? What are the marks of an unhealthy church? How do you move a ministry from "un-health" toward health and productivity?

POWER

As Christian leaders, you and I are responsible to move people God-ward, but none of us is powerful enough to change anyone else's life. That realization frees us to be servant leaders.

Practically, how does our "theology" become "biography"? How do we go beyond agreeing with Jesus to seeing transformation in our own lives and in others?

There is a tension between personal ambition and a calling from God. Personal drive and ambition need to be re-shaped by God. Ego must diminish, and human visions have to be harnessed or removed. Self has to be displaced into serving God's agenda, not our own.

PERSONALITIES

Is self-care biblical? If it is, what is involved in biblical self-care? How is biblical self-care different from setting boundaries?

Chapter 8: Conflict – The Achilles Heel of Ministry .. 75

Most strains and ruptures in ministries are not theological or differences over vision. They are relational. Conflict is inevitable and unavoidable. Conflict is a fork-in-the-road. It is a hands-on opportunity for the Lord to bring personal and inter-personal growth if we respond in Christ-pleasing rather than God-grieving ways.

Chapter 9: Building Teams 93

Healthy leadership teams do not happen easily or by accident. How do you build healthy teams?

PRACTICE

Chapter 10: Boards as Overseers 105

Biblical leaders are mature people who have been shaped by life experience to firmly trust and follow God, His purpose, and His ways. They become point people who verbalize, mobilize, and organize people-movement God-ward so that people come to know and grow in Christ.

Chapter 11: Plans and Progress 117

Vision is only good intention until it is turned into action. Practically-gifted task people shine in identifying and carrying out the details of whom, how, and when in order to turn vison into reality.

Chapter 12: Alignment 123

APPENDICES

PREFACE

"I want to write a book." I was a young pastor in my late 20's, two years into my first pastorate. Ray, a seasoned friend and mentor, smiled and placed his hand on my shoulder as he said, *"But you don't have anything to say yet."*

That was 35 years ago. In those 35 years, I have served two permanent pastorates, and am currently serving my 15th intentional interim pastorate with churches in transition or crisis. I have pastored churches of varying sizes, ages, demographics, and denominations. I have had the privilege of coaching Christian leaders, training groups of emerging leaders, and coming alongside indigenous leaders in the two-thirds world.

I love the church of Jesus Christ. More precisely, I love what the church is meant to be as the body of Christ in the world. The late E. V. Hill urged us to *"be who you is, 'cause if you is who you ain't, you ain't who you is."* That challenge – to be who you is – also applies to the church. The church is meant to live out its Jesus DNA. Yet too many churches and Christian ministries are not *"being who they is"* biblically.

As Howard Hendricks noted, *"I have never met a Christian who sat down and planned to live a mediocre life."* Yet many Christ-loving committed leaders are weary and settling for simply doing the job. And dedicated volunteers sacrifice time and money yet wind up frustrated and worn out.

I am convinced that second only to the moving of the Spirit, competent, biblically-grounded leadership is the next most vital factor in healthy fruitful ministry. "Leading well" does not guarantee results – nothing can – but competent, biblically-grounded leadership markedly increases the odds of healthy, sustained, Christ-honoring ministry.

This book is for Christian leaders, whether in the ministry or in the marketplace.

How do we experience the fingerprints of God upon us and upon the ministry He has given us? *Leading Well* is arranged by sections — the Purpose, Power, Personalities, and Practice of "leading well" as a Christ-like servant leader.

I have written this book to spark renewal in your own life, while equipping you to lead well in ministry. I hope you will experience a caring arm around your shoulder and a firm hand in the middle of your back as we discover what it means for leaders to help Christian ministries meet the challenge of their calling. Our calling is worth it. The world for which Jesus gave His life needs the body of Christ to be who it is, because *"if it is who it ain't, then it ain't who it is."*

Paul J. Murphy
Apple Valley, Minnesota
February 2017

www.progressandjoy.net

Additional leadership resources available at www.progressandjoy.net:
- One-to-one leadership coaching
- Servant Leader Boot Camp — group training available in video format
- Church Check-Up — congregational process assessing health and clarifying core direction

PURPOSE

CHAPTER I
God's Unchanging Purpose

"The church is dying for lack of leadership." George Barna

God only needs leaders for one unchanging purpose. Without exception, the biblical evidence about leadership unfolds a consistent picture – God only appoints leaders for one, unchanging purpose.

I am the son of an Irish-Catholic immigrant. At the age of two years old, my father immigrated with his parents to the United States. I was raised in a moderately religious home. We attended mass regularly. During my teen years, I felt an increasing inner restlessness. I constantly wondered, *"How can I get closer to God? If God is real,"* and I believed that He was, *"shouldn't He be more alive, more exciting than this?"* God seemed like a long-distance phone call with a bad connection, or a soft drink without the bubbles. Shouldn't there be bubbles with God? And what was I supposed to do about my own failings and feelings of guilt? The inner pull to be closer to God – and the brake pedal of guilt and fear – created stress inside me. I was longing for relationship with God, with no idea how to find it.

The Lord is masterful at reaching us where we are. For me that meant sports. During the first week of high school, the

Lord placed a new friend and teammate in my life. I remember Rob asking me, *"Would you like to have breakfast in a gym with 300 high school kids and listen to a guy give a chalk talk?"*

As a basketball player the word "gym" always caught my interest. A gym packed with 300 high schoolers sounded fun. A guy giving a chalk talk sounded weird. The gym turned out to be his church gym. The 300 teenagers were the church youth group. And the chalk-talk guy was the youth pastor. As I stepped across the threshold into the gym that first Thursday morning, I clearly sensed that the answer to a relationship with God was in that gym. The caring of others and the clear simple messages from the Bible drew me like a magnet. Thursday mornings became a highpoint in my week.

During that year I came to understand that Jesus died for a relationship with me, the costly proof that God loved me and was seeking me even more than I longed to know Him. In every sense of the word, this was good news to my confused, searching heart.

As part of coming to personal faith in Christ, I felt an irresistible tug to help others know Him. If I only had one life to live on earth, what could be better than spending it as a mid-wife between God and people? Through various jobs, college, and marriage, the draw of serving Christ in vocational ministry never faded. After completing college and three years working in sales in the business world, I was off to seminary, and the senior pastorate.

Yet twelve years into pastoral ministry, I was pleading with the Lord to release me from my call to ministry. I poured out to the Lord, *"I love the church, but it is killing me."* I was burned out and depressed. Our church leadership group had been gridlocked for years. Like a car spinning its wheels on ice, we had lots of friction but no forward progress. I was weary, wounded, and disheartened. Having tried everything else, I resigned. This was not how I expected ministry to turn out. *What happened?*

Sadly, my experience is not unusual. Many of my classmates from seminary are no longer involved in vocational Christian ministry. This wounded-in-action syndrome is not limited to those in vocational ministry. It is also an all-too-familiar painful reality for volunteer leaders in many churches and Christian organizations. Talented, Christ-loving lay leaders, successful in their secular work, agree to serve in positions of volunteer leadership in a ministry only to become discouraged and frustrated. Frequently I would ask a gifted lay person to consider serving in leadership, only to have that person, or his or her spouse, look at me with a pained face or cynically laugh as he or she said, "*No thanks, I won't be doing that again.*" *What happened?*

In the western world we are awash in resources. There is an abundance of seminars, training courses, and books. Many pastors and lay leaders are struggling to lead and sustain healthy, productive lives and ministries. Too many churches are unhealthy environments and are plateaued or declining. At the same time the culture is moving away from Christ, or at least away from the church. *What's happening?*

My own pain and burnout drove me to ask a simple question — what does the Bible say about leadership? I embarked on a personal journey through God's word. Beginning in Genesis and ending in Revelation, I noted every passage that referred to leaders, leading, or leadership. I read the stories of leaders, both good and bad, in Scripture. Like the popular *CSI* crime shows, I wanted to "go where the evidence leads me".

3

The same patterns about leadership kept showing up again and again. Like pieces fitting together in a jigsaw puzzle, a picture was clearly emerging for me. Without exception, the biblical evidence about leadership reflected a consistent picture – biblically, God only appoints leaders for one, unchanging purpose. Regardless of culture, point in history, type of ministry, our purpose as Christian leaders never changes. God always enlists leaders in His work for one single reason – moving people God-ward.

> **God only needs leaders for one unchanging purpose – moving people God-ward.**

Abram was called to be a blessing to nations (Genesis 12:1-3), which is echoed again in Psalm 67. In Jesus's first message, He declared, *"The Spirit of the Lord is on me, because he has anointed me to proclaim good news to the poor. He has sent me to proclaim freedom for the prisoner and recovery of sight for the blind, to set the oppressed free, to proclaim the year of the Lord's favor"* (Luke 4:18-19). He commissioned His disciples to *"go and make disciples of all nations"* (Matthew 28:19-20).

Translated literally the apostle Paul describes the church as the fullness of Him who is progressively filling everything everywhere with the knowledge of himself (Ephesians 1:22-23). The church is God's plan for continuing the ministry of Jesus by loving and reaching people (Matthew 28:18-20, Colossians 1:28-29, 1 Thessalonians 1:8-10). In the final book of the Bible we read, "After this I looked, and there before me was a great multitude that no one could count, from every nation, tribe, people and language, standing before the throne and before the Lamb. They were wearing white robes and were holding palm branches in their hands. And they cried out in a loud voice: 'Salvation belongs to our God, who sits on the throne, and to the Lamb.' " (Revelation 7:9-10).

Like a funnel, the biblical stories of leadership flow in one direction, toward a single purpose of moving people God-ward. As Christian leaders, we are in the people-moving business. Are you engaged in Christian leadership? Then you are in in the people-moving business. Whatever your role, your core purpose is moving people God-ward. Some of us are used by the Lord to move people to choose first-time faith in Jesus Christ. Some of us may be used by the Lord to move people further in discipleship, a life of knowing and following Jesus. Whatever your specific role – managing, administrating, or serving on a governing board, leaders are to MOVE PEOPLE GOD-WARD into relationship with Him!

Moving people God-ward is the magnetic North Pole for Christian leaders.

Even children understand singled-minded focus and purpose. When my son Mike was in third grade, one of his assignments was to write a short essay titled, "If I were President I would..." Here is what he wrote:

> *"If I were President I would make things easier for kids. Some kids cannot afford to buy toys. Next I would give $1 million dollars to the zoo and to Kids' Camp. Then I would bring virtual reality to all 50 states. Finally, I would give each kid [15 and younger] $15 cash. Then I would resign."*
> Mike M.

As a third-grader, my son had a clear focus. As president he would be about one thing – helping kids. If you were not a kid, you were not part of his focus as president.

The Bible is a love story

God too is captivated by one driving purpose. His heart beats for relationship with us. Incredibly, the Creator has chosen not to be satisfied apart from relationship with us! He longed for it enough to act by taking on our human flesh and blood in Christ. He is so determined to be in relationship with us that Christ literally died for it.

The Bible is a love story of God's amazing and relentless pursuit of relationship with us, no matter how long it may take or what it may cost Him.

> **Moving people God-ward is the unchanging magnetic North Pole for Christian leadership. As Christian leaders, we are in the people-moving business.**

For the last 21 years, I have worked with churches in crisis or transition. That means I work with unhealthy, hurting congregations. What separates healthy from unhealthy ministries? Healthy churches know they are a means, not an end. They live as a conduit, being the body of Jesus in the world. When church becomes an end, a congregation is already unhealthy. The only question is how sickness will surface in that church.

I was invited to work with a church that wanted to identify a new vision for their future. One key theme that surfaced from congregants was a desire to reach more young families in the community. I asked, "*Why do you want to reach more young families?*" Their answer grieved me. They smiled and replied, "*To keep our church going."* Their motive was keeping the church going. The survival of the church had become their purpose. Their church had become an end in itself. Within a few years that church closed its doors. When a church becomes an end in itself, the congregation is unhealthy.

Unhealthy churches have mutated into self-preserving organizations. Their commitment to go and give away themselves and the love and truth of Jesus to the world has diminished next to preserving the existence of their church. Churches focused on attendance, finances, conflict avoidance, and keeping the doors open and members satisfied are unhealthy. When church becomes the purpose – rather than living as a means of moving people God-ward – then church becomes an idol.

In contrast to this, on the outskirts of St. Paul Minnesota is a 130-year old church. The neighborhood had dramatically changed during previous decades. Today the neighborhood is a mix and match of various ethnicities and family make-ups – some single parent households, some living together unwed, some same sex unions, and some traditional families.

Most of the church's members commuted from outlying suburbs. Half the church members were seniors, with a number of them living as shut-ins or in nursing homes. The average age of the church was increasing faster than real time. They were wrestling over their future as a church. As these dear people came together in prayer, fear, and faith, they came to a shared conclusion – they needed to become a church of the neighborhood. They hired a person of color on staff. They reached out with practical love and care to the needs of the neighborhood. They began seeing people of the neighborhood move God-ward. Their commitment to moving people God-ward was greater than their self-preservation instincts.

Recently I had the joy of working with a large flagship church. The church had a rich history, but it had drifted into maintenance mode. Using Church Check-Up, a congregational participation process that I developed, we involved the entire congregation in constructively assessing the current spiritual health and clarifying the future direction for the church.

The result was renewal as church members recommitted themselves to being a means of moving people God-ward. They determined to equip themselves to become mobile missionaries where they live, work, and play. Their focus shifted from maintenance mode to deploying Christians in their community to love and reach people for Christ, and to grow them up in a relationship with Christ.

Jesus came and gave Himself away – loving, teaching, suffering, and dying for the world. He commanded us to "*go and make disciples*" throughout the world. Nowhere is the world commanded to come to church.

As Christian leaders, we are in the people-moving business. God's heartbeat is relationship with people. The one and unchanging purpose for Christian leaders is moving people God-ward. His body, the Church, is to be a means of moving people worldwide into relationship with God.

Reflect and Act

1. How did the Lord use others to move you to a relationship of faith in Christ? List their names, and how their lives moved you God-ward.

2. As a leader, how is your heart? Are you weary? If so, what is wearying you?

3. Has your church or ministry become an end in itself? Or is it a means to spread God's love by moving people God-ward?

   • Is your church's approach "come to us," or does your church "go" into the world? (*List some concrete examples.*)

   • What stories are most shared in your church? (*List some concrete examples.*)

4. How might an intentional focus on moving people God-ward influence:

   • Your attitude toward to whom you minister?

   • To whom you minister?

5. What you are spending your time doing with people?

6. As a leader, are there any adjustments or changes you need to make so that moving people God-ward is your main heartbeat and focus?

   • Is there anything you need to stop doing?

   • Is there anything you need to start doing?

Partner

Share your responses with another leader. Pray together about what stands out to you from your responses.

Dig Deeper

Use the Scriptures in Appendix A to freshly connect with God's heart for relationship with people, and with your own role in moving people God-ward.

PURPOSE

Chapter 2
God's Unchanging Purpose and You

"Learn to love someone when they least deserve it, because that is when they need your love most." Rodolfo Costa, *Advice My Parents Gave Me: and Other Lessons I Learned from My Mistakes*

Your life as a leader is a message and a ministry. The good news gospel of Jesus is life-changing. It will change us, and change how we treat others. How Jesus treats us is to become how we treat people. The Vertical is to become the Horizontal.

The gospel is God's good news of invitation to relationship with Himself. As we respond and move God-ward, it changes our heart, our attitudes, our habits, and our relationships. Life has a new trajectory as our "theology" – what we believe is true about God – becomes "biography" – impacting and transforming us.

Leadership is about more than skills and strategies. Your life as a leader is a message and a ministry. Is there God-ward movement in your own life? How are you closer to the Lord than six months ago? Than a year ago? How is your theology transforming who you are and how you live? Do you love people? Does your heart ache and break for others to have relationship with God?

The fingerprint of Jesus was love. It is the new commandment (John 13:34). It is the evidence of God's Spirit in my life (Galatians 5:22-23). It is the goal of Paul's ministry (1 Timothy 1:5). Without love anything we do for Christ has no value (1 Cor. 13:1-3). The Bible does not merely say that God "loves" but that God IS love (1 John 4:8). It is not just what He does, it is who He is!

Imagine if we conducted a survey of the public and asked one question – "*What is your impression of Christians?*" What do you think the survey results would reveal? Would the public describe their perception of Christians as: busy or available; issue-driven or people-centered; critical or caring; closed-minded or good listeners; smug and hypocritical or serving and compassionate; detached or serving; judgmental or sacrificially serving? Or, would the survey reveal the public has no impression of Christians at all?

Remember the uncomfortable encounter in John 4 between Jesus and a Samaritan woman at the well. The disciples are absent. It is just Jesus and the woman. In first century culture, Jews had no dealings with Samaritans. Each despised the other, viewing the other as heretics to be avoided. Jewish men would not be alone with a woman, especially a Samaritan woman. And this particular Samaritan woman is an immoral woman. Divorced multiple times, she currently has another man in her life but is not married to him.

Kindly and deliberately Jesus engages her in conversation. He stirs her curiosity and gently confronts her failings. He reveals Himself to her as the promised Messiah. Movement God-ward takes place in her life! She goes and tells her fellow Samaritans about Jesus.

Looking at her, Jesus did not see a sinful failure to be judged or avoided. Yet His disciples, His closest followers, failed to "see" what Jesus saw. They were surprised (the word in Greek means unsettled, disturbed) that Jesus was alone with the woman. They saw the woman as someone to be avoided. Jesus challenged their faulty way of seeing people, *"Open your eyes and look at the fields! They are ripe for harvest."* (John 4:35).

For those of us who embrace God's love in Jesus, who bask in a restored relationship with God, has it changed how we "see" others? Do you see every person through Christ-eyes? "Seeing" people with new eyes will change how we treat them.

Splachna acts

The father in Luke 15 is moved with compassion toward his prodigal son. The word compassion is the translation of the Greek word "*splachna.*" *Splachna* means moved in your gut. The father was so deeply moved that he was compelled to act. He moved toward the person for whom he felt compassion. The father literally moves – running across town, sobbing and embracing his returning son, and hosting a celebration feast. *Splachna* acts.

"Compassion" is the same word used to describe the Good Samaritan's responses to the man beaten and left for dead along the Jericho Road (Luke 10:25-37). Religious leaders travelling along the same road each "saw" the beaten man. They may have felt sympathy for the beaten man, but only one person was moved in his gut to act. Only one, the Samaritan, showed *splachna* – compassion that moved him to action to help a wounded stranger.

13

Simon is one of my friends, a fellow minister for Jesus. Simon lives in Uganda where motorcycles called *boda boda* are used as inexpensive taxis. Simon was hurrying to get home before the coming of the heavy rains. He approached the *boda boda* driver for a ride. Along the side of the road was a poor woman, a Muslim, walking toward her village. Simon knew she would be drenched in the coming downpour. His heart was moved with compassion for the woman. Simon gave his money to the *boda boda* driver and told the driver, "*Take this woman to her home.*" She arrived in her village just before the heavy rains began, saying to her fellow villagers, "*A man of God helped me get home, but he was not a Muslim.*" Simon's treatment of the Muslim woman became a reflection of Christ's love to her entire village.

> **Compassion – *splachna* – is sympathy moved to action.**

Sympathy is a feeling. When we see something that troubles us, or if we feel sadness for a person suffering, that is sympathy. Compassion is sympathy moved to action. Seeing our sinful brokenness, God has *splachna*. He could have turned away in disgust and ignored us. He could have vented His anger over how we have offended Him. He could have lectured us, issuing a shape-up-or-else ultimatum. He could place us on some form of probation. He could have judged us, imposing consequences, a spiritual version of the timeout chair. Instead He acted with compassion by moving toward us, becoming one of us. Rather than being repelled by our failings, He drew close to people. He loved and befriended sinners, He DIED for messy, flawed, sin-infected people!

GOD
COMPASSION OF JESUS

Has God's life-changing love in Jesus gotten hold of you and moved you God-ward? If so, is compassion becoming how you now "see" and treat others? How is your *splachna*?

The "Vertical" – how the Lord treats us in Christ – is to become the "Horizontal" – how we treat others. That is the essence of Christian maturity. Jesus' great commandment zeroes in on the Vertical – *"Love the Lord your God"* – lived out through the Horizontal – *"Love your neighbor as yourself."* The cross forms this visual – vertically, God's love reaching down to us, and then horizontally, reflecting that love to others around us. Ministry is messy. We are meant to move <u>toward others </u>with love in the face of their brokenness and sinful failings. I love Paul's challenge in Ephesians 5:1-2, *"Imitate God, therefore, in everything you do, because you are his dear children. Live a life filled with love, following the example of Christ. He loved us and offered himself as a sacrifice for us, a pleasing aroma to God"*.

> **The Vertical is to become the Horizontal –**
> **that is the essence of Christian maturity.**

My wife and I were part of a monthly book club with several other couples in full-time ministry. When it was our turn to host, I was eager to share my insights about the book we had all read. The book selection was C. S. Lewis' *The Problem of Pain*. I could not wait to tell the group how I was smarter than

C. S. Lewis. As I proudly blurted out my discoveries, the room fell silent. Quickly one couple after another excused themselves and found reasons to leave early. Too late I realized to my disgust that I had turned all of our guests off. I had literally cleared the room with my arrogance.

I felt the self-loathing described by Jackson Browne in his song *Your Bright Baby Blues,* when he wrote, *"No matter how fast I run I can never seem to get away from me."*

My wife Liz sat down next to me on the sofa. She placed her arm around me, looked deeply into my eyes, and calmly said to me, *"I HATE that about you, but I LOVE you."*

In the face of my worst foot forward, she conveyed love to me. She did not ignore or minimize my ugly behavior. She faced it, and still moved toward me in love. That act of love, in the face of my arrogance, gave me hope. If she could still love me in spite of my pride, then I could get up and try to keep growing again tomorrow. The next day I contacted each couple from our book club, apologizing for my attitude.

How Jesus treats us is to become how we treat people. The Vertical is to become the Horizontal.

GOD
COMPASSION OF JESUS

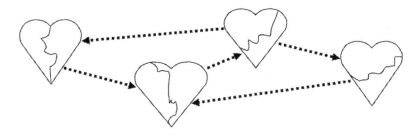

The first pastorate I served was a small congregation of 90 people in southern California. The church had a reputation as a "consumer church" – one that consumed its pastors. The church had been static for years. It was rare to see someone come to a newfound faith in Christ. A handful of us began praying that we would become a church body that was reaching people who did not yet know Christ.

Several weeks later a visitor paused to speak with me. She expressed interest in being part of a small group, telling me, *"I have never read the Bible. I am struggling with alcoholism and depression. If God cannot help me I may not be able to go on with life."* She offered to host a gathering in her home to explore the basic messages of the Bible. She offered to invite her neighbors, who were as or more messed up than she. A group of 8 to 10 of us gathered regularly.

That home group became one of the most delightful groups I have had the joy of leading. Over the next few years we came to know one another well. There was pain and failure in each one's story. There was also a longing to find a relationship with God. We learned together, prayed for one another, ate meals together, and helped one another. Over time many of them came to a personal faith in Christ. It was messy, and it was wonderful. It was where Jesus would have spent His time.

The world is meant to experience the life-changing *splachna* love of Jesus through us. The Vertical of God's love for us is to become the Horizontal of how we move toward and love sinfully-broken people with His loving compassion.

Reflect and Act

1. *How has this Chapter impacted you?*

2. *How is your* splachna *toward others, particularly those who do not yet have a relationship with Christ?*

   - *How are you responding when you come face-to-face with the sinful brokenness of others? Are you seeing them through Christ-eyes, or as people to criticize or avoid? Cite a recent example in your own life.*

   - *Is there a person or a group of people you find hard to truly love?*

   - *Who can you move toward with love and grace? Be specific.*

Partner

Share your responses with another leader. Pray together about what stands out to you from your responses.

Dig Deeper

Read Luke 10:25-37, and John 4:1-42.

PURPOSE

Chapter 3
Healthy and Unhealthy Churches

"Church activity is a poor substitute for genuine spiritual vitality. We have made following Jesus all about being a good church member. We are training people to be good club members, all the while wondering why our influence in the world is waning." Reggie McNeal, <u>The Present Future</u>

God's heart is for relationship. Our purpose as Christian leaders is moving people God-ward. What is a healthy, productive church? What are the marks of an unhealthy church? How do you move a ministry from "un-health" toward health and productivity?

I passionately believe in church. But I believe in a healthy, productive body of Christ, not in an anemic, unhealthy church. I have spent 35 years of my vocational life gladly giving my time, energy, and heart for the church. I am a turnaround guy. I work with churches and leaders in transition and crisis. I have served 17 churches (15 as an intentional interim pastor), and coached and trained hundreds of pastors and lay leaders from a variety of denominations in the United States and overseas in underdeveloped countries.

What are the marks of healthy and unhealthy churches? How do you move a ministry from sickness toward health and productivity?

A major, influential church was marking its 25th anniversary. It was a historic moment. The congregation had reserved the city's professional sports arena that seated over 12,000 people. Worship was wonderful. I expected that the pastor felt big expectations to deliver a landmark message. As the pastor stepped to the podium, he began to speak, "*What kind of church do WE want to be?*" He repeated it again, more loudly, "*What kind of church do WE want to be?*" As I recall, he voiced the question a third time even more loudly. I turned to my wife and whispered, "*I am leaving. Do you want to come with me?*" She was confused. "*But he is just starting his message.*" "*I know,*" I replied, "*but he is asking the wrong question. The question should be what kind of church does Jesus want His body to be.*"

In fairness, the pastor may have gone on to speak about what kind of church Jesus wants His body to be in his sermon. But his opening sentence pushed a button for me. The church is not "our" church. The church is the body of Christ in the world. The question is not, "*What kind of church do we want to be?*" The question is, "*What kind of church does Jesus desire His body to be?*" The issue is ownership. The church belongs to Jesus. What does He intend? What matters to Him?

If you were asked to summarize the heart and message of Jesus in a single word, what word would you choose? What word did Jesus Himself choose? As I read the gospels, the single word that distills Jesus' ministry is "life." Jesus said, "*I am the bread of life… I am the resurrection and the life… I came that they might have life abundantly....I am the way the truth and the life."* Near the conclusion of his gospel, this is what John wrote, *"Jesus performed many other signs in the presence of his disciples, which are not recorded in this book. But these are written that you may believe that Jesus is the Messiah, the Son of God, and that by believing you may have life in his name."* (John 20:30-31).

Healthy, productive churches see themselves as a means to a greater end. As the body of Christ, their passion is to see Jesus' Kingdom furthered on earth, to see people moving God-ward.

Unhealthy churches

Unhealthy churches have made the church an end in itself. They have unintentionally substituted "church-ianity" for "Christ-ianity." The "un-health" of church as an end surfaces in different symptoms.

I remember feeling uneasy, as I prepared to begin working with the next church as an intentional interim pastor. At its height this church had more than 600 people attending Sunday services. Now, after a painful division over keeping or terminating the pastor, the church was shell-shocked – down to 200 in attendance. Worse still, the atmosphere among the 200 was frosty. It was like a divorce when neither the husband nor the wife is willing to move out of the house, both insisting, *"It is my house, why don't YOU leave!"* Many congregants literally sat on separate sides of the sanctuary. On one side was the group who had supported the pastor, while those who had voted against the pastor sat on the other side. Was this church too divided, too far gone to turn around and become a healthy body again? Was this church beyond recovery? Divisions and ruptured relationships had become the focus, even the identity

21

of this church – painful evidence that it was an unhealthy church.

In another church I was invited to be part of a church assessment team. The congregants were blaming the church problems on the last pastor, the elders, and the denomination. As part of the assessment we conducted interviews with the people of the church. Over 80% of those interviewed cited a handful of troubling realities, including distrust of the elders, poor conflict resolution, lack of direction, and an inward clique-like environment. The denomination insisted the church spend at least twelve months with an intentional interim pastor before they hired a permanent pastor. The church contacted me, asking if I would consider serving as the intentional interim pastor. I agreed to serve.

I began visiting with congregants. Person after person would say to me, "*I still think we are a good church.*" I was stunned. How could they possibly feel that they were "still a good church" in the face of the interview results that revealed high levels of un-health and discontent?

Over time I understood it. Their own identify was tied to the church. They had given their heart, their time, and their money to this church for decades. To admit the church was unhealthy would be admitting they personally were not spiritually healthy. Their own identity had become linked to the church's image. The church had become an idol in their lives. They were manifesting another sign of unhealthy churches, a preoccupation with image preservation.

Another church I served as an intentional interim pastor appeared fine on the surface. However, busyness had replaced purpose. Even busyness for Christ can be another symptom of an unhealthy, inwardly-focused church. Like Martha busily doing activity, there are churches that have become beehives of activity. They fit the old joke about the airline pilot saying, *"Ladies and gentlemen, I have good news and bad news. The good news is we are making record time. The bad news is I have no idea where we are going."* Activity is not the same as productivity. Activity can mask un-health. Rollo May noted, *"It is an ironic habit of human beings to run faster when we have lost our way."*

> **Unhealthy churches have made
> the church an end in itself.**

Each of these churches had detoured into the church being an end in itself. When the church itself becomes an end, it is already unhealthy. The more church is the focus of our conversation, energy, and relationships, the greater the symptoms of ill health. Is the atmosphere marked by pride — what a great church we are? Or is it marked by unresolved feuds and conflicts? Both are symptoms of a self-absorbed ministry that has morphed into making itself an end.

The church is meant to be like a gas station. When was the last time you pulled into a gas station with a mini-market and spent the day there? You fill your car with gas, and clean the windows. Perhaps you even check the air pressure in your tires. Maybe you buy a snack or newspaper. You pay. Do you then sit down, get comfortable, and spend the rest of the day visiting with the folks in the mini-market? Instead, we get into our cars and drive off down the road. We know the purpose of a gas station mini-market is to fill up so that we can get back on the road toward our destination.

Unhealthy churches have turned the church into an end destination, rather than an equipping, refueling stop that helps believers get back on the road to their destinations in life and ministry.

When church is the focus, then fellowship, too, can easily become an end in itself. Like a cul-de-sac that we circle round and round but never exit, we can produce Christians who are merely hothouse plants. The New Testament lays out about 35 different "one another" commands. Relationships with fellow believers are vital for our growth in Christ. That has certainly been true in my own life. What if we viewed fellowship as a lab? A lab is where we put theory into practice. A lab is where we learn by doing, testing, practicing, and correcting. The same is true for sports or theater. Practice and rehearsals develop skills so that an athlete or a performer is at his or her best on game-day, or when the curtain goes up for a live performance.

In other words, the "one another" commands are a way to help us learn through practice how to live out the new life in Christ, so that it becomes our daily lifestyle in how we treat fellow believers and not-yet-believers. Fellowship is not just how believers are to treat one another. Fellowship sharpens and develops us so as we live in the world, we are salt and we are light. As I practice and experience caring, forgiving, resolving conflicts with fellow believers, I become caring, forgiving, and a peacemaker in all my relationships. The world sees and experiences Christians putting on the "new man" of Christ.

The way back to health

Jesus underscored this concept with His new commandment in John 13:34 *"So now I am giving you a new commandment: Love each other. Just as I have loved you, you should love each other. Your love for one another will prove to the world that you are my disciples."*

24

Faith and love were the two signs of healthy life that Paul repeatedly looked for in churches. When sincere faith in Jesus and love shown to others were apparent, Paul affirmed them. He then built upon that foundation to mature them in Christ.

Jesus spoke of pruning in John 15. Pruning hurts. Pruning is embarrassing. Pruning looks bad. It feels like we are going backward, not forward. Jesus prunes us so that we will bear more fruit, thereby proving to be His disciples. (See John 15:1-12.) James and Hebrews agree – pain and hard times are meant to mature us in Christ. How we respond to the pain determines if fruit will be produced.

Pain can become the doorway to renewed health. There are many causes of pain in this fallen world. The Lord is not the author of all pain in our lives. Yet I am convinced that regardless of the source of the pain, the Lord intends to use pain for good and for growth in our lives. That is one of His unique claims to fame – like a master recycler, He can use and bring good and gain out of anything, and everything.

During hard times I frequently remind myself of Hebrews 12:11, *"No discipline seems pleasant at the time, but painful. Later on, however, it produces a harvest of righteousness and peace for those who have been trained by it."* The phrase "trained by" is the Greek word *gumnazo*, from which we get our word "gymnasium." In other words, trials are like a personal trainer to help us get in better shape. Our part is to cooperate with the workout God is permitting in our lives. We are to allow ourselves to be trained by it. When we do, pain becomes constructive. It becomes "growing pains," rather than simply pain. If we ignore pain in our lives, or adopt a self-pitying victim attitude (Hebrews 12:5), then we miss the gain from pain that God intends for us.

25

In your own life how are you cooperating with the painful pruning the Lord is using to grow you up? How as a church or ministry are you cooperating with, rather than ignoring or fainting from, trials that God intends to use to mature you?

**Jesus prunes us so that we bear more fruit,
proving that we are His disciples.**

Swimming laps is my main form of physical exercise. As I was finishing my workout, I could see parents with their young children gathering on the poolside deck about to begin a beginning swimmer class. One five-year-old boy was hugging his father's leg as he said, "*I am really good up to here,*" pointing at his chest. He was already anxious about being in water over his head. He preferred the security and control of being able to touch bottom while standing up. He feared going into the deep end of the pool. He honestly admitted his fear of being in over his head. If his father allowed him to stay in shallow water only, the boy would never develop as a swimmer. The father enrolled his son in swimming lessons so he would mature as a swimmer, rather than spend his life in the shallow end of the pool.

We are a lot like that five-year-old boy. That is why our Father enrolls us in the school of trials, so we mature and grow up in our faith. Life is a classroom. Are you paying attention? Are we cooperating with the growth the Lord intends in our lives?

In John 5, Jesus encounters a man who has been lame for 38 years. Jesus asks the man a short, penetrating question, "*Do you want to get well?*" I cannot find another time when Jesus asked someone that question. Did the lame man truly want to grow and see his life change, or had he formed an identity around his disability? Did he want to get well, or did he want sympathy without change in his life?

The same question applies to churches and ministries experiencing pain and trials. Do we want to get well?

Like a person resisting going to the doctor, individuals and ministries often avoid an honest look in the mirror. The sad price-tag for excusing, blaming, and avoiding is that no gain comes from the pain. It is wasted pain. Spending your energy, personally or as a ministry, assigning blame, denying your problems, pretending things are not so bad, saving face, etc., means you will not gain from the pain. You will not get well.

Blaming problems on the former pastor, or on the elected leaders, or on a lack of commitment by the young people, or on an unwillingness to change by the older people, or on the building, or on the denomination, etc., are excuses to avoid looking in the mirror at ourselves. The sad result is you will not gain from the pain. You will not get well.

Productive pain that brings God-pleasing fruit emerges from a humbled heart. Humility is the gift no one wants, yet it is the gateway to experiencing renewed health. Humility breaks us, opening us to inviting the Lord to bring His health into our tired, hurting lives. James 4:6 offers a wonderful promise, *"God opposes the proud but gives grace to the humble."* David got gain from his self-inflicted pain, *"You do not desire a sacrifice, or I would offer one. You do not want a burnt offering. The sacrifice you desire is a broken spirit. You will not reject a broken and repentant heart, O God."* (Psalm 51:16-17). Twice David used the Hebrew word "broken," which means fractured, crushed, broken, in pieces, smashed. Humility hurts. Yet the Lord allows us to break so we come to the end of ourselves and turn to Him to remake us.

> **Humility is the gift no one wants, yet it is the gateway to experiencing renewed health.**

Recently I walked with a church through their pain toward the gain God brought into their lives. The church had grown rapidly during its ten years. Then, the pastor resigned and started another church nearby. It was as if a roadside bomb had been detonated, inflicting emotional, relational, and spiritual shrapnel wounds. People were confused and angry. Some left, searching for a new church home. Others, disenchanted, simply gave up on church. The church began a downward spiral. Attendance dropped over 50%. Finances also dropped. Morale and hope were at low ebb. One person who chose to leave the church said to me, *"Paul, this is a race to the bottom."* For most people, grief and an impending feeling of gloom became the mood.

As their intentional interim pastor, I too was in pain. I was feeling heaviness and despair. I remember sharing with a colleague and friend, *"I have tried everything I know to do, and this church is still not turning around. I can't fix it. It is like a ship that is still leaking and taking on water."* It was the most difficult of my fifteen interim pastorates.

Frustrated and feeling useless, I knelt in the living room and told the Lord, *"Send someone else. I am not the right person for this church."* The Lord gently impressed upon me, *"Paul you are right where I want you."* I insisted again, *"No, Lord, send someone else."* Again, I sensed the Lord telling me, *"Paul, you are right where I want you."* A third time I poured out my weariness and frustration to the Lord saying, *"Lord, You are not hearing me. I do not want to be here. This is wearing me out. Send someone else."* I sensed the Lord asking me, *"Paul, where are you RIGHT NOW?"* I looked around me and replied, *"I am on my knees, praying to You."* It clearly hit me. That was where the Lord wanted me, on my knees, depending upon Him, not myself, to move this church.

As I rose from my time of prayer, I felt a weight lifting from me. I felt able to continue loving and leading that hurting, discouraged church. The pain was carving humility within me.

During those months I found encouragement reading and rereading I Thessalonians. The apostle Paul cared deeply, and yet he realized that failure is an option. He wrote, *"Our visit to you was not a failure.... I was afraid that the tempter had gotten the best of you and that our work had been useless."* (I Thessalonians 2:1 and 3:5) Failure is an option. I felt free. If the Lord wanted this church to close down, then it would close down, and I would not be able to stop it. And if the Lord wanted this church to continue, then nothing could close it down.

We pressed on, serving in faith, trusting the Lord, not ourselves, for the church's future and health. We were humbled. We felt weak. We held tightly to the Lord amidst our pain. And that church began emerging from its grief. Painful pruning began producing fruit. Hope returned. People who felt they were in over their heads experienced God's goodness and faithfulness as they hung on in humility and faith. Fruit came. The church has continued to recover and rebound, more mature in Christ from its pain. Months after I concluded my work as their intentional interim pastor, I continue to hear from active members about the recovery and progress of this church. Here is what one of them recently wrote to me, *"As I sat in church today with a fully packed sanctuary I couldn't help but see the fruits of what God has done in our church. With the Lord's help, you healed a hurting congregation. You gave us a vision and helped us move forward. I see so much excitement and promise."*

29

I miss those dear friends in Christ. Whenever I am in southern California and have a free weekend, that is the church I enjoy returning to visit. When we humbly cooperate, the Lord brings gain and fruit from the pain of life.

The apostle Paul always looked for faith and love as the indicators of spiritual health. I see this repeatedly in churches and leaders who are moving from unhealthy to healthy. Difficulties produce a humble faith that shows itself in a fresh turning and submitting to Jesus as our Lord and Head. Out of the humility birthed by pain, believers return to Jesus as their sole source of unity. They freshly seek and submit to Jesus' will, rather than insist on having their way. Prayer increases. Forgiveness and resolving conflicts replace blame and distrust. Love for others returns. Health emerges from humbly cooperating with pain.

Maybe we need a bumper sticker for those of us who live a life of faith in Jesus that simply says, *"Fruit happens!"*

Reflect and Act

1. How do you respond to the image of church as a gas station, rather than as an end in itself? Is the focus of attention on church (church-ianity)? Make a list of concrete examples:

   - List examples that are indicators that our church it is "an end" in itself.

   - List examples that are indicators that our church is "a means" to reaching the world.

   - As you look at your 2 lists above, is the ministry you are engaged in out of balance? If so, what changes need to be made?

2. Do you agree that fellowship is meant to train us how to treat all people, not just believers? How are you living out the "one another" commands with each person in your daily life?

3. How are you responding to trials and pain in your own life, and in your ministry? Write down the trials you are living with right now.

   • Are you responding in humility, cooperating with the gain the Lord intends, or are you blaming and ignoring, i.e., avoiding taking an honest look in the mirror?

   • How can you cooperate with the growth the Lord intends through your trials?

4. What "fruit" do you see, or sense the Lord bringing, in your own life? In your ministry? Intentionally look for it – it is the evidence of the Lord bringing gain from your pain. It brings hope to your hurt.

Partner

Share your responses with another leader. Pray together about what stands out to you from your responses.

Dig Deeper

Read John 15:1-12, Hebrews 12:1-15, and James 1:2-12.

POWER

Chapter 4
Responsible But Not Powerful

"God made man because He loves stories". Elie Wiesel, <u>The Gates of the Forest</u>

"I'd rather be sailing...pray for wind." Bumper Sticker

As Christian leaders, you and I are responsible to move people God-ward, but none of us is powerful enough to change anyone else's life. That realization frees us to be servant leaders.

It had been a bad day. For that matter it had been a bad week. That morning I had been criticized by a congregant for being too dictatorial. That same afternoon a family informed me they were leaving the church because I was a pushover. As they put it, *"You are too much of a marshmallow."* It left me frustrated and second-guessing myself. If only I had been more aggressive. Maybe I should have been more patient. Or perhaps, if I had just said things differently, talked more or talked less, listened longer, or been more assertive?

I poured out my sadness and self-doubt to my wife. Looking me in the eyes she said, *"Wow, you must be a really powerful man!"* This seemed like an odd way to be supportive. She continued, *"Do you honestly think that if you had done everything just so, and said everything just the right way, that everyone would get in line and go along with you? Are you that powerful? Who do you think you are?"*

There it was – a helpful, loving whack upside the head. She had reminded me that we cannot change others. We are not powerful enough to control another person's attitudes, actions, or beliefs. That is humbling. It is also freeing.

As leaders, our purpose is moving people God-ward. Yet within ourselves we do not possess the power to make people move God-ward. We are responsible, but not powerful.

There is profound theology in the bumper sticker, *"I'd rather be sailing....pray for wind."* Rowing a boat is about effort – human exertion, sweat, and toil.

In contrast, the sailor depends on the outside power of the wind. Sailing is about partnering with a greater power – the wind.

If you were stranded on a deserted island and could only have a few pages of Scripture, what part of the Bible would you want to have with you? I would take 2 Corinthians 3-5.

The Apostle Paul describes the powerful inner working of the Spirit in 2 Corinthians 3-5. In 2 Corinthians 3:3 he says, "*You are a letter from Christ, the result of our ministry, written not with*

35

ink but with the Spirit of the living God, not on tablets of stone but on tablets of human hearts."

He writes in 2 Corinthians 3:4-5, freely admitting that he is not competent (meaning "capacity," "power," or "ability") to change anyone's heart. Instead, he declares in 3:6, "*The Spirit gives life.*" The new way of a changed life by the Spirit surpasses the old way of rules and commandments delivered by Moses. In 3:17-18, Paul lays out the work of the Spirit as a work of freedom and transforming people more and more into the glorious image of Christ. The word he uses for transform is the Greek word *metamorphosis*, meaning an actual morphing; a genuine changing of what a person is like. He is not yet done telling us about the work of the Spirit inside people's hearts and minds. The Spirit is the "*power*" (the Greek word is *dunamis*, from which our word "dynamite" comes) that creates "*a new person*" in Christ. (2 Corinthians 4:7, 5:17)

Paul relied upon the Spirit, not himself, in his ministry. He was responsible, but he knew he was not powerful enough to change anyone's life. Paul served in love, messaged the good news of relationship with God through faith in Jesus, and viewed people through Christ's eyes (2 Corinthians 5).

Paul saw himself as a servant, and the Lord as the One who is the Power that impacts hearts (2 Corinthians 4:5-7). In 2 Corinthians 4:7, Paul says, "*We have this treasure in jars of clay to show that this all-surpassing power is from God and not from us.*"

This all surpassing power is from God and not from us. There it is, both humbling and freeing for you and me as leaders in Christ's work.

As leaders, we are responsible but not powerful.

I have the privilege of devoting a portion of my time to training Christian leaders in less developed countries, what is sometimes termed the "two-thirds world." Twice a year I travel to Uganda and Ghana to work with young leaders. Pallisa is in a rural part of eastern Uganda. Several decades ago three men hopped on very used bikes and pedaled over 40 miles each way on dirt roads. Their goal was to ask a Christian evangelist to come and help start a church in Pallisa. He did. Today over 30 churches have come out of that little church in Pallisa. Of the different churches I work with in Uganda, the Pallisa church may be my favorite. The dear people and sweet aca-pella African singing and warm smiles of joy always move me.

Those three men acted in faith. The result of their faith was a powerful working of God's Spirit. If you asked them how they did it, they would smile and tell you that the Lord did it.

The three men of faith who biked (left to right) along with one of their sons, next to the church-planting evangelist (right)

Jesus' own words about the Spirit are often misunderstood and misapplied. "When he comes, he will prove the world to be in the wrong about sin and righteousness and judgment: about sin, because people do not believe in me; about righteousness, because I am going to the Father, where you can see me no longer; and about judgment, because the prince of this world now stands condemned". (John 16:8-11)

Some wrongly assume this means that God's Spirit is going to get unbelieving people and make them miserable for not believing in Jesus. The word "convict" means to convince, to persuade to the point of accepting or believing.

Look again at Jesus' words about the Spirit's work. The Spirit will convince people they are sinful, that Jesus is God's Sent-One, and that the devil has been defeated. That sounds like good news, not bad news. That is the work of evangelism, not judging. One verse earlier in John 16:7, Jesus says: *"But in fact, it is best for you that I go away, because if I don't, the Advocate won't come. If I do go away, then I will send him to you."*

The Spirit filled the gap left when Jesus departed earth. The Spirit carries on the same work Jesus did when he was on earth. Jesus is clearly saying that His Spirit is the Power – the convincer, the persuader, the power that changes peoples' hearts and minds. The Spirit works within people to move them God-ward! That is the Spirit's job description – changing hearts, moving people from ignorance and unbelief to faith and new life in Christ.

In the beginning the Lord created the heavens and the earth, the physical creation all around us. He has not ceased being an artist. He is still creating, but the canvas and focus of His creating work is the inner person, through His powerful Spirit working in hearts and minds.

As leaders, we are responsible but not powerful.

Rick was one of the most successful lawyers in the upper Midwest. By his own admission he had it all – money, women, success, and security. Yet he had an inner restlessness that literally sent him on a global quest searching for the meaning of life. He visited our church one day, and we agreed to have lunch. During lunch he told me, *"I feel really good about my relationship with God as a Father, but I cannot accept this stuff about Jesus dying on a cross as payment for my sins."* Here was a brilliant guy asking me to explain to him the good news of Jesus! Tapping into my seminary training, I used my best illustrations and made a clear presentation of the gospel.

I ended with a big finish asking Rick: *"Can you think of any other way that God could remain just – punishing sins, while also being loving toward us, other than His love and justice intersecting in the Person of Jesus dying on the cross?"* I expected Rick to say, *"That is what I have been waiting to hear, thanks for making it clear for me, yes I see it all clearly now."*

Instead, Rick said, *"Yes, I can think of at least 5 other ways God could have handled things."* He began articulating alternate ways God could be just and merciful. He said, *"If you give me some time I can probably come up with more."*

I was frustrated and angry, not with Rick, but with the Lord. My presentation of the gospel had hit a brick wall and bounced back with seemingly no impact. I had done my part presenting the clear message about Jesus. Why had it not sunk in with Rick, who wanted to believe?

I climbed into my car, fuming about God not showing up. By a God-coincidence I had been given a recording of a message promoting an upcoming citywide prayer gathering. As I drove home from the lunch, I listened to the recording. The message was a bulls-eye aimed right at me. The speaker had three points as I recall: (1) Life is a spiritual battle, not merely a human effort; (2) You cannot change anyone else's mind; and (3) We are utterly dependent on God's Spirit to do spiritual work in the lives of others. His theme was: Are you self-reliant or Spirit-reliant? I realized I was trusting in ME to move Rick to faith in Christ. I began praying for Rick.

Three months later I asked if he would like to meet for lunch again, to which he replied, *"Yes, I would love to. I want to tell you about my relationship with Jesus."* I was speechless. Apparently in a recent sermon I had made a brief side reference to Isaiah's statement referring to Jesus as "wonderful, counselor, mighty God, everlasting father, prince of peace." Rick told me, *"When I heard that it all became so clear – that was Jesus!"* Rick's mind and heart changed at that moment. He willingly chose faith in Christ as God's unique Sent-One who died for him. Rick became a follower of Jesus, using his talents to serve a number of Christian causes.

You and I are responsible to move people God-ward, but none of us is powerful enough to change anyone else's life. That realization has been freeing for me. It has freed me to serve and share Christ without feeling stress. It has freed me to be straightforward and clear in presenting the gospel, just as it did for Paul (see 2 Corinthians 4:1-7). It has freed me to pray more and to trust God's Spirit, not myself, to change the lives of those I care about.

The power of the Spirit rather than self-reliance also has something to say to us collectively. Are we trying to make the ministry work, relying on our education, or experience in business, or the latest book or seminar? That may mean we are rowing in our own energy, carrying the burden on our shoulders for the ministry turning out well.

I can painfully remember meeting with a key leader in a church I had just begun serving as the intentional interim pastor. As he reached out to shake my hand, he introduced himself saying, "*I am the guy who wrecked the church.*" He held an important job in corporate America. During follow-up visits he shared with me that when the church he loved was struggling, he took it upon himself to lead and fix it, using his business experience. The results were not what he had hoped for, as more pain and ruptured relationships ensued.

I believe humanly "church" does not work, and God intended it that way. If we in our own energy and experience try to run the church, it will not work. A muscular, well-dressed body is still shockingly ugly if it is decapitated. A headless body is a horror. It will be a headless body. As the body of Christ, we are meant to cling to the Head, Jesus, rather than humanly trying to make church work (Ephesians 4:15-16).

Are we consciously and regularly depending upon the Spirit to bring about heart-softening, genuine love, change, and growth – the "fruit of the Spirit" that both Jesus and Paul spoke about (John 15 and Galatians 5)?

Are you rowing or sailing? Sailors know they are dependent on the wind to move the boat. Sailors know they have a part to play – trimming sails, manning the rudder, studying the weather pattern, etc. In the same way we still have a role to play –to serve others in love, to share clearly the good news of life in Christ, and to trust in the power of the Spirit to change hearts and lives.

"I'd rather be sailing…pray for wind."

Reflect and Act

1. *Do you relate more to the rowboat or sailboat leader? Why?*

2. *What change and growth is needed in your own life? Be specific.*

   • *Invite the wind of the Spirit to "morph" you, rather than strive to change yourself.*

3. *Is there a person like Rick in your life, who you have been trying to reach for Christ?*

   • *How does this Chapter help clarify your role and the Spirit's role in moving them God-ward?*

   • *What practical effect will it have upon you and how you approach ministering to others?*

   • *Like the men on bikes from Pallisa, do you need to take a step of faith in serving the Lord?*

4. *How do you react to the statement, "Humanly church does not work, and God intended it that way?"*

   • *What are one or two steps your ministry can take to become more Spirit-dependent, rather than man-reliant?*

Partner

Share your responses with another leader. Pray together about what stands out to you from your responses.

Dig Deeper

Read John 16:7-11, and 2 Corinthians 3-5.

POWER

Chapter 5
How Transformation Happens

"All our theology must eventually become biography." Tim Hansel, <u>You Gotta keep Dancin</u>

Practically, how does our "theology" become "biography"? How do we go beyond agreeing with Jesus to seeing transformation in our own lives and in others?

A young adult friend of ours is not fond of church. She accompanied a friend to an emergent church service. Later that night my cell phone rang. She said, *"The pastor said, 'Jesus was a revolutionary, and if you are going to be a follower of Jesus, then you must be part of a revolution. I like that!'"*

Jesus was a revolutionary. The much loved beatitudes are actually a call to a radically new way of living and doing relationships. Look at the people Jesus spent time with – broken, sinful, diseased, failures, and outcasts. Even in choosing His apostles, Jesus was revolutionary. He chose unlearned "dropouts" from the educational system. And within three years His unlearned followers were changing the world in a chain reaction that is still growing globally 2,000 years later.

Take a few minutes and read again through the beatitudes of Jesus in Luke 6:20-49. This is a radical way of living. Following

Jesus is meant to impact everything – our attitudes, our relationships, our money, our values ... everything!

One morning I was peering over the wall of my hotel in eastern Uganda. Two women with primitive wood-handled hoes were tilling a large plot of dirt. For three straight days I saw them straighten up and lift their hoes overhead, then bending at the waist, swing the hoes downward sinking them into the fertile soil. Then they would stand upright and push the hoe forward to break up the dirt before lifting it overhead again, to once again swing it into the rich red soil. Backbreaking, slow work. By the end of the third day they had finished tilling a large plot of land, preparing it for seeding before the coming rains.

The next day I was on the road training Ugandan pastors in a rural area. I posed a question to them, *"In Uganda I see that most of you have a farm plot. Can you tell me, how did you learn to farm?"*

One by one, Ugandan men eagerly stood to proudly tell me how they learned to farm. Each gave the same explanation – *"When I was a child my father took me with him out to the farm plot. He handed me a hoe and had me stand next to him. I watched him hoeing and I began to do as my father did. My father would correct me when I did it wrong, showing me how to hoe properly. And that is how I learned to hoe a farm plot."* The women added, *"That is how I learned to cook, too – my mother took me with her to pick food, and then I stood by her as she peeled and cut and cooked it."*

I asked them, *"Did any of your fathers stay in the house and tell you to pick up a hoe and go outside and hoe the farm plot?"* They laughed at how silly this suggestion seemed to them. I then asked, *"Why as Christian leaders we do a lot of telling and are surprised it does not produce changed living?"* We began talking about how we as leaders can help people learn to hoe their spiritual garden.

Jesus was a master teacher. He did more than simply transmit information to His disciples. Jesus spoke truth in the context of relationships along with putting the disciples to practical action. All three – truth, relationships, and action – are needed for transformation.

Transformation = Truth + Relationships + Action

Truth

Look again at Jesus' words at the close of the beatitudes in Luke 6:46-49. It is not the one hearing but the one acting on Christ's words that sees a marked difference. The same pattern is repeated in the parable of the four soils in Matthew 13:1-23. All four soils "heard" but only one of the four experienced productivity.

I dislike our popular term "Bible study." Bible study might produce smart, knowledgeable believers but not necessarily healthy, mature believers. We can slip into believing that knowing what the Bible says is the mark of a mature follower of Christ. For many of us, we may do well to chew our Bible food longer. Slow down the volume of Bible reading. Invest more time consciously applying what truth we have been learning until it is woven into our living.

During a week stay in Poland I chose to do a simple daily spiritual exercise. Each day I would meditate on one aspect of the fruit of the Spirit. Numerous times throughout the first day I would remind myself, *"The fruit of the Spirit is love."* As I was sitting in a café eating, I would recite again, *"The fruit of the Spirit is love."* When I walked down the sidewalks, or browsed in a shop, or waited in line for a tourist site, or passed people on the street – numerous times during that day – I simply repeated that phrase, *"The fruit of the Spirit is love."* I became aware of how short-lived and shallow my "love" for others was. At the end of the day I found myself praying, *"Lord, I am not really very loving of others, deepen my love."*

The next day I meditated on *"the fruit of the Spirit is joy."* Repeating that phrase throughout the day, I became aware of how much I lack a heart of joy. The third day the same thing happened as I pondered *"the fruit of the Spirit is peace."* Many times during the day I was not at "peace."

That simple exercise of slowing down and reflecting on God's truth in the midst of my daily living helped me apply God's truth in my thinking, attitudes, and actions.

These days I have been doing the same discipline with Psalm 84. Each morning for the last six weeks I recite from memory the entire psalm. I take time to let it speak to me. More than information, it is getting inside my heart, my emotions, and my will. Does my whole being have a homesick longing to be in God's presence (Psalm 84:1-5)? God offers joy, grace and glory, favor, and good things for those who turn God-ward (Psalm 84:8-12). Even difficulties and a feeling of being far from God are ways to deepen our longing for Him (Psalm 84:2-7).

Relationships

An isolated Christian is not a growing Christian. God uses others to further our growth in Him. There are over 35 different "one another" commands in the New Testament. Paul's prayer in Ephesians 3:18-20 is in the plural. You could correctly translate it "you all."

> And may you [plural] have the power to understand, as all God's people should, how wide, how long, how high, and how deep His love is. May you [plural] experience the love of Christ, though it is too great to understand fully. Then you [plural] will be made complete with all the fullness of life and power that comes from God. Now all glory to God, who is able, through his mighty power at work within us, to accomplish infinitely more than we might ask or think. Glory to him in the church and in Christ Jesus through all generations forever and ever! Amen.

Part of how we experience Christ is together in community with others.

In Haiti I had the delight of training young emerging Christian leaders. As I entered the room I was wearing a dirty, smelly, torn shirt. I was teaching from Ephesians 4 about *"putting off the old man"* and *"putting on the new man in Christ."* Frank was providing translation into Creole. Frank turned to me and said, *"Let me help you Paul."* He tugged the dirty sweaty shirt off over my head. He then placed a fresh clean shirt on me. That is the picture Paul lays out in Ephesians 4 and elsewhere. We are to help one another grow up in our life in Christ. The commands are in the plural. Hebrews 12 is plural as it urges us to *"strengthen your feeble arms and weak knees. Make level paths for your feet, so that the lame may not be disabled, but rather healed."* (Hebrews 12:12-13) In other words, growing up in our faith is a team, not an individual, sport. We are to help and support one another.

47

We need one another for growth and transformation. We do not grow and mature in isolation. The "one another" life is a shared life. With whom do you share your joys, needs, questions, struggles, and needs? With whom do you extend care, giving your time and possessions to help them?

Yes, relationships can be messy and will at times let us down. Jesus stepped into relationships. He formed a learning community of His disciples. None of them was called to a life of individual discipleship. Their call was lived out in relationship with one another.

Action

"Truth" plus "relationship" plus "action" produce transformation. It is how Jesus discipled His followers. He taught truth, involved them in relationship with one another, and sent them out on learn-by-doing action assignments.

A few years ago a knock at our front door was the beginning of one of the richest relationships of my life. Tim, our neighbor across the street, stood at my door asking if we knew "the people in the blue house." Tim informed us that Jon, a 34-year-old man in the blue house had been diagnosed with stage-4 cancer, and was in the hospital undergoing major surgery.

I went to visit Jon in the hospital the next day. As I stood outside his hospital room door, I wondered what I would encounter once I pushed open the door. It was to be the beginning of a wonderful friendship. I walked through the door and saw six people surrounding my neighbor Jon as he lay in his bed. We visited for 15-20 minutes. As I prepared to leave, Jon asked me if I would say a prayer.

After he was released from the hospital, Jon phoned me and said, *"They tell me faith is an important part of beating cancer. Would you write a prayer that I can recite each morning and evening?"*

I drafted a prayer, and we sat down to talk about it. Jon was appreciative. He seemed eager to learn more about the sections from Scripture that I had included in the prayer. We began meeting regularly to read and discuss the Bible. Jon's faith relationship in Christ came alive. His appetite and love for God blossomed before my eyes. About two months later Jon was scheduled for another surgery. He asked if I would write another prayer for him. I declined, saying, "We have been looking at God's Word together for the last six weeks, Jon. Why don't you write your own prayer this time and we can talk about it together". Jon wrote a lovely, honest prayer. We continued meeting together – sharing, praying, and growing in our friendship and in our relationship with Christ. Jon maintained an amazingly positive, determined attitude during his struggle with cancer. I recall Jon's desire to share Christ with other cancer patients.

Other neighbors expressed interest in what Jon and I were doing. What began as Jon and me meeting together weekly, grew into a neighborhood bi-weekly Bible discussion group of eight to ten neighbors who were learning, sharing, and moving God-ward in their lives.

That April there was a knock at my front door. There stood Jon. He knew that my mother was struggling with a health illness and that her birthday was May 5. Jon smiled as he said, *"I have an airfare voucher I cannot use. I thought I would give it to you so you can go see your mom for her birthday."*

On May 4 I was on a plane bound for southern California to spend three days with my parents. We had a wonderful visit. My father commented, *"Your mother hasn't laughed like that in years."* On May 6 I said good-bye to my parents and boarded a plane back to Minneapolis. Two weeks later my mother unexpectedly passed away. None of us, not even the doctors, expected this. How kind of the Lord to send me on a final, joyous visit to see my mother just days before she passed away. After my mother's death I connected again with Jon, telling him, *"Jon, the Lord used you in a significant way in my life. For the rest of my life I will always be grateful to you and the Lord for your gift of the trip out to visit my mother."* He was surprised and overjoyed to learn the Lord had used him in my life.

Jon optimistically and energetically battled his cancer for four years. Just days before he passed away he said to me, *"If I can just get this stomach pain under control I think I will be good to go."* Jon and I both gained and grew in our faith from one another.

My friend Jon was literally across the street from me. What if I had not visited him in the hospital? I would have missed a deeply meaningful relationship. Jon would have missed experiencing a living relationship with Jesus. Our neighbors would have missed the opportunity to explore faith in Christ.

Jesus said, *"Open your eyes and look at the fields! They are ripe for harvest."* (John 4:35) There are people "ripe" for the good news of Jesus within your reach. They are waiting for us to put our faith into action by loving, befriending, and sharing Jesus with them.

Small Groups

Small groups are a staple in most churches. Yet how Jesus led His small group was markedly different from how many of our churches do group life today. Jesus had a rhythm of three ingredients in discipling His small group: **truth, relationship** with one another as a learning community, and **action** by serving others, including those who are not yet people of faith. If our goal is to grow disciples, let's follow Jesus' own approach.

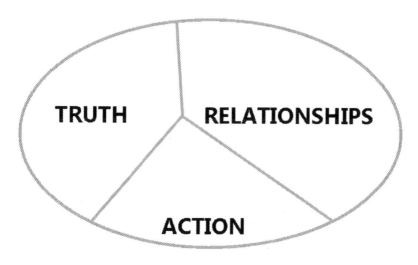

Truth

Is your small group learning truth from God's word with practical, personal application? Are you sharing stories of growth in one another's lives in your group? Is growth happening as you tap, use, and develop the talents of people in your group, rather than one leader doing it all?

Relationships

In your group life, do people feel welcome, accepted, and safe to be honest? Does your group give and receive support through attentive listening, encouragement, experience-sharing, wisdom, and prayer for one another? Does the group act to meet practical needs?

Action

Beyond limiting ourselves to serving other believers, how does your group practically act in care for not-yet-believers? What could your group do to put outreach to not-yet-believers into action?

What if we asked those in our group a simple question, "*Is there anyone in your circle of relationships – at work, in your neighborhood, from social connections – who does not yet know the Lord, but is in need of that knowledge life right now?*" Which of those persons will your group come around by showing and sharing the good news of God's love in Christ? Rather than adding an extra time commitment, make one of your monthly group meetings going and serving that person or family who does not yet know Christ. In other words, weave outreach action as a rhythm of your group life.

To separate outreach-evangelism from discipleship is to re-define and distort discipleship in a way that Jesus would not recognize or affirm.

Relational outreach and evangelism

I see some churches recovering Jesus' approach in making disciples. They combine truth plus caring relationships plus action that embeds relational outreach and evangelism as part of discipleship.

Jesus' regularly engaged His disciples in outreach actions and relationships. One cannot read the gospels without easily realizing that much of Jesus discipleship approach was involving his followers in hands-on shoulder-rubbing experiences with people who thought, lived, and behaved quite differently from their own Jewish beliefs. These days the home screen on my cell phone is a photo of a shrine to the mythical god Pan that is carved into the hillside in what in Jesus' day was the pagan town of Caesarea Philippi. It was in Caesarea Philippi that Jesus asked his followers, "*Who do people say that I am?*" and "*Who do you say I am?*," to which Peter declared, "*You are the Christ, the Messiah.*" Jesus chose a pagan city, not a city within Jewish culture, to conduct this crucial conversation with His disciples. It was one more signal that reaching out to those who are not yet people of faith was central to Jesus' mission for His followers.

Outreach and evangelism are part of the very fabric and model of discipleship that Jesus lived out. (I define "outreach" as acts of love, mercy, and justice with those who do not yet know Christ. I define "evangelism" as verbalizing (putting into words) the good news gospel message about Jesus Christ with those who do not yet know Him.) When we morph "discipleship" into simply time spent with other believers, studying Scripture, praying for one another, and serving within the church, we have mutated discipleship into something that Jesus would not recognize or endorse.

The Church Check-Up process engages the entire congregation in assessing the health and direction of the church. I frequently see congregants rating their church weakest in local outreach and evangelism. The issue is deeper than simply creating more activities for churchgoers to invite not-yet believers to come and hear the gospel.

Since discipleship as Jesus lived it is a lifestyle that includes outreach and evangelism, we as his followers need to make outreach and evangelism part of how we disciple people.

53

Appendix E is the summary report from one church that made a conscious decision to embed outreach and evangelism as a lifestyle among its people, so that outreach and evangelism became a way of life. This means growing believers into missionaries where they live, work, and play.

Like a good parent, God desires transformation – not mere information – for His children. Becoming more like Jesus happens when we live out His truth in relationships with others, including those who do not yet know Christ.

Reflect and Act

1. In your own spiritual life, is there a combination of Reflecting on Truth + Caring through Relationships + Serving through Action?

   - Is there a balance of all three?

   - Are you out of balance in any one area?

   - What changes do you need to make?

2. In your ministry, are you intentionally developing disciples by Reflecting on Truth + Caring through Relationships + Serving through Action (including serving not-yet-believers)? In your discipleship approach:

   - To what extent is there a balance of all three?

   - Are you out of balance in any one area?

   - What changes do you need to make?

3. Utilize Appendix B as a resource to guide and evaluate your discipleship programs.

Partner

Share your responses with another leader. Pray together about what stands out to you from your responses.

Dig Deeper

Read Luke 6:20-49, and 2 Corinthians 3 to 5.

POWER

Chapter 6
Ambition and Calling

"If anyone wants to come after Me, let him deny himself, take up his cross and follow Me." Jesus

"He must increase, and I must decrease." John the Baptist

There is a tension between personal ambition and a calling from God. Personal drive and ambition need to be re-shaped by God. Ego must diminish, and human visions have to be harnessed or removed. Self has to be displaced into serving God's agenda, not our own.

The best pastor I have known is Walt. Walt was warm, caring, intuitive, and creative. He was a gifted communicator and a highly effective leader. He was immensely respected. He pastored an upper-class congregation of over 3,000, the largest church in his denomination west of the Mississippi. Yet he once told me that *"the hour I most dread is Sunday morning when I have to preach."* Walt went on to tell me he had agoraphobia (fear of open or public places). If he had things his way he would be restoring vintage cars instead of pastoring a church. Being who he was, Walt shared his struggle with panic attacks with his congregation. Others with similar phobias came forward and shared their struggles. A number of them voluntarily sat in the front rows as a silent support group for Walt as he delivered his sermons.

It is difficult to find a single example of a good leader in the Bible who sought the role. None chased his or her role. Repeatedly we see God interrupting and re-directing people's lives. They were responders to God's call, not initiators. God initiated disruption, a "calling," that resulted in their obeying His leading. The list is long – Noah, Abram, David, Esther, Jeremiah, the Minor Prophets, the disciples of Jesus, Paul, and on it goes.

In each case, following God's call cost them. In every case it meant risk. For some it meant giving up the comfort of the familiar, for others giving up financial security, or geographically relocating. For others it meant ridicule and suffering. In many cases it meant literally risking their lives.

Personal drive and ambition need to be re-shaped by God. Ego must diminish, and human visions have to be harnessed or removed. Self has to be displaced into serving God's agenda, not our own.

Moses had the passion and vision of liberating the Israelites from Egyptian oppression. His strong sense of social justice and personal ambition led him to take the initiative to make it happen – with disastrous results. The ambitious would-be revolutionary leader spent the next 40 years as a fearful fugitive hiding out on the backside of nowhere tending sheep. It was to the failed, fearful Moses that God appeared in the burning bush. God's vision of liberating the Israelites from Egypt was much the same vison that Moses tried acting on decades earlier. Moses in his failing and fleeing has become a far different man. A broken, reluctant servant-leader now emerges, rather than a man serving his own agenda (Exodus 2:11-4:23).

The story of zealous, ambitious Saul and his transformation into Paul parallels Moses. He first had to be knocked flat on his back and rendered temporarily blind, humbled, and helpless, in order to serve God's call. Intense ambition and "driven-ness" had to be broken, and harnessed into servant leadership.

Humble leaders are not indifferent or less determined. Humble leaders in Scripture cared deeply and sacrificed significantly. But they served God's agenda, not their own ambition. John the Baptist understood this when he said in John 3:30, *"He must become greater; I must become less."*

The essence of sin

I am convinced that much of the Lord's work in our lives is removing self as the center of our hearts. It is inner work. It is heart-surgery work by the Spirit.

The essence of sin is that self has displaced the Lord as the center. Self is the most insidious and dangerous idol. Jeremiah 17:9 warns us, *"The heart is deceitful above all things and beyond cure. Who can understand it?"* Jesus hit this head-on in Mark 8:34 when He declared, *"Whoever wants to be my disciple must deny themselves and take up their cross and follow me."*

For centuries people wrongly believed the earth was the center of our solar system. Galileo was tried as a heretic for proposing that the sun, not the earth, was the unmoving center of our solar system.

Adam and Eve exchanged a relationship of dependence and trust in God for self-centeredness. Self replaced God as the center of their inner universe. All of us are born infected with that same flaw. Our preoccupation with self exposes how we have placed self, rather than the Lord, at the center of our lives.

> **The essence of sin is that self has displaced the Lord as the center. Self is the most insidious and dangerous idol.**

After serving two pastorates over a period of 12 years, I was burned out. I had become anxious and depressed. I had trouble sleeping. My dear wife suggested that I might need to go and see a clergy counseling specialist. I told her I would think about. She replied, *"Don't think too long. You have an appointment tomorrow morning, and I am driving you to it."*

I resigned that pastorate. I found myself with a knot-like ball of anger trapped in my gut. I was angry at God for letting me down, for leading me into vocational ministry, and then allowing me and my family to become abused, worn out, and wounded. Where was God when I needed Him? But pastors are not supposed to be angry with God, are they? Few people understood my struggle. And few wanted to hear about it.

While I was wrestling with my pain and anger, I was also job hunting. I was certain that the Lord would open the door for another pastorate. Instead, an opportunity with a faith-based non-profit serving at-risk youth presented itself. During the interview process Fred, the Executive Director, stared at me and said, *"It is very important you feel called to this job. Do you feel "called?"* I paused and replied, *"When did Joseph feel called to Egypt?"* I was somewhere I did not plan or even want to be as a result of brothers letting me down. Looking at me, Fred said, *"You are hired."* He understood what it felt like to be Joseph. Fred became for me a role model of a humble servant. There were other people I met in my Egypt-like experience who became living role models of serving and following Jesus. There were lessons to learn about myself and about leadership. There were new skills to be acquired that have been of lasting value. Most importantly, there was needed soul surgery the Lord was doing within me.

Although I was a believer in Jesus, I slowly and painfully began to see that my identity was grounded in what I did for Christ, rather than my identity being in Christ. The Lord was chiseling away at my most deceptive and cherished idol – self. It was painful surgery. It was wrenching. It was wonderful. It was freeing. I came to deeply appreciate Paul's two-word phrase "in Christ." Far more than a prepositional phrase, "in Christ" is synonymous with new life, a new identity, and therefore a new way of living. In his letters Paul labored to help early believers grasp and live out their new identity in Christ.

In his book *Mourning Into Dancing*, Walter Wangerin describes the birth experience from the vantage point of the emerging newborn. Everything is changing, out of control. Noise, squeezing, bright lights, the loss of the safe amniotic sack all seem to the distressed newborn like dying, not birth. In the same way, removal of self-centeredness is a painful death-like process. On the other side, however, is a new kind of life. A free life. A life in Christ as our settled, joyous experience.

In the hard times of our lives we too easily can focus on who was at fault, or wonder "why me," or look for sympathy from others. Warren Wiersbe titled one of his books *The Bumps are What you Climb On.* What if we put our theology into practice – reminding ourselves "God can cause good to come from this?" What if we viewed our trials, frustrations, and even our failings through a new set of eyes? As a loving father, God intends to grow us up, to transform us. Like a master recycler He uses everything including trials for our good and our growth.

None of us is exempt from trying times, including Jesus. He was arrested on false charges, tried and found guilty by a

61

mock court, unfairly tortured, and then crucified as a criminal though He was guilty of no crime. God took and used all that evil and suffering and caused it to work for good – turning the cross of Christ into a story of hope and power and a triumph of His love. For that to happen Jesus had to trust God more than he cared for self.

Getting gain from pain

There is a marked difference between pain and brokenness. Brokenness – humility - is the gift no one wants. There is no waiting in that line.

Imagine falling off the curb and breaking your leg. You are screaming in pain and clutching your damaged leg. A bystander runs over and says, "*I am a doctor, I can help you.*" If you reply, "*Do not touch my leg,*" then you are in pain, and there will be no gain from the pain. But if you instead reply, "*Do whatever it takes to save my leg,*" that is an attitude of humility that sur-renders and trusts.

> **Brokenness – humility - is the gift no one wants. There is no waiting in that line.**

There is nothing attractive about being pruned. Pruning hurts. Pruning can be embarrassing. Pruning can feel like we are going backward, not forward.

Down the street from my parent's home, one of their neigh-bors is an impressive gardener. Roses are his passion. Walk by and you will see tall and short roses, large and small roses, roses of many different colors and fragrances. The front yard is like walking through the rose section of a nursery.

As I was out walking one morning I noticed the neighbor's front yard looked different. All his roses were cut back. Instead of the beauty of colors and fragrances I saw sticks and stumps. Not a rose was in view in the front yard. Stooped over, the neighbor was gathering the rose branches he had trimmed into a trash barrel. As I passed by I commented to him about pruning his roses. With a weary voice he said to me, *"Yes, and it better be worth it because this is a lot of work."* Several months later I again was visiting my parent's home and went out for a morning walk. The neighbor's front yard was a burst of color and fragrances – roses in bloom. It was indeed worth it.

Jesus said "I prune" so that you will "bear more fruit" that will glorify the Father. (John 15:1-12) Fruit – becoming more like Jesus– is what the Lord intends to bring from painful pruning. But pruning requires that we cooperate in order to gain from the pain.

People whose response to trials in their lives is bitterness, blaming others, or feeling sorry for themselves get no fruit from the pain.

Hebrews 12:11 reminds us, *"No discipline seems pleasant at the time, but painful. Later on, however, it produces a harvest of righteousness and peace for those who have been trained by it."* Will you just choose to scream in pain, or will you cooperate, allowing the Lord to prune away self and ambition and weakness, to shape you more into living as the "new man in Christ," rather than the old self-centered sinful man?

Pruning in order to bear more fruit also happens in the church. I have had the privilege of working with a number of churches in crisis or transition. All were in pain, experiencing moderate to severe pruning. Confusion was high. Relationships were struggling. Morale was low. Hope was down.

How the church responded determined if the congregants gained from the pain. Churches in pain that looked for someone to blame, that excused their troubles rather than being willing to take a look in the mirror, did not gain from their painful trials. Those churches that responded in faith, turning freshly to the Lord in a healthy humility of brokenness, emerged with renewed unity and closeness to the Lord, and a fresh energy to serve Him. Cooperating by looking to what the Lord was doing through their pain transformed pain into "growing pains." They got the gain from the pain. Fruit happened!

Reflect and Act

1. Can you see your painful experiences as a kindness by God as He prunes away ambition and weans you from self-love?

   - How ambitious and driven are you to succeed?

   - Are you too concerned with what others think of you – gaining their approval, or fearing their disapproval?

   - Is your identity "in Christ," or in what you do for Christ?

2. How are you responding to the pain of trials in your life?

   - How are you (or can you) cooperate with what the Lord is doing?

   - Are you preoccupied with blaming, being bitter, seeking sympathy, or other unfruitful responses?

3. Is the Lord at work pruning the ministry of which you are a part?

   • As a church body or ministry organization, how are people responding?

   • What from this chapter could help your ministry to gain from its pain?

Partner

Share your responses with another leader. Pray together about what stands out to you from your responses.

Dig Deeper

Read John 15:1-12, Hebrews 12:1-15, James 1:2-8, and James 4:1-10.

PERSONALITIES

Chapter 7
Biblical Self-Care

"Very early in the morning, while it was still dark, Jesus got up, left the house and went off to a solitary place, where He prayed."
Mark 1:35

"Your actions are speaking so loud I cannot hear what you are saying."
Anonymous

Is self-care biblical? If it is, what is involved in biblical self-care? How is biblical self-care different from setting boundaries?

J. Oswald Sanders commented (from Leadership, Vol. 7, No. 3):

It is possible to throw our lives away foolishly by burning the candle at both ends. When Robert Murray McCheyne, only thirty years old, lay dying, he said to a friend at his bedside, 'God gave me a message to deliver and a horse to ride. Alas, I killed the horse, and now I cannot deliver the message.' The horse was, of course, his body. Christian workers should accept it that their service will be costly if it is to be effective, but they should be careful not to kill the horse.

In the process recently of rolling over my IRA, my financial advisor asked me how much longer I planned to work. He noted that if I could delay drawing any retirement income until after age seventy and a half, I would earn more per month. Financially it makes more sense for me to work at least until age seventy and a half. Plus, I really enjoy what I do vocationally. I often tell people that I am blessed to do what I love and twice a month I even get paid for it.

The main factor that could prevent me from working full-time into my seventies is poor health. I am responsible for my health. No one else will exercise for me, rest for me, or eat well for me.

In the Old Testament, *shalom* was the by-product of being in right relationship with the Lord. More than just peace, *shalom* meant an overall state of well-being, effecting emotional, mental, physical, social, and spiritual well-being. In short, an overall peace-of-mind, peace-of-life.

Self-care is not selfish nor is it optional. Self-care is a stewardship responsibility. Our bodies are a temple in which God lives (1 Corinthians 6:19 and 2 Corinthians 6:16). Staying in shape – mentally, physically, emotionally – is taking care of that temple. It is a stewardship issue, being responsible with what God has entrusted to my care. Self-care is not self-indulgent. It is biblical and necessary. It reboots us and our relationship to the Lord and to our role in His creation.

Sabbath

Sabbath is a break from the routine and grind of daily life. It was initiated by the Lord Himself. Genesis 2:2-3 says, "*By the seventh day God had finished the work he had been doing; so on the seventh day he rested from all his work. And God blessed the seventh day and made it holy, because on it he rested from all the work of creating that he had done."* Do any of us really believe the Lord was "tired" and needed the rest? He was modeling the value of regularly breaking to rest from the daily demands and work routine of our lives.

In the gospels Jesus had a habit of regularly stepping away from the demands and pace of His daily life. Mark 1:35 describes one occasion, *"Very early in the morning, while it was still dark, Jesus got up, left the house and went off to a solitary place, where He prayed."*

Christian service can become an excuse for work-a-holism, for never pressing the off button. When we do not practice self-care, including Sabbath, we open the door for eroding consequences. Our families can feel secondary to ministry in our lives. We become more susceptible to burnout or pride. If we are too busy to practice healthy, biblical self-care, we distort the meaning and message of the gospel. While our words may communicate a gospel of grace and acceptance, our work-a-holic actions communicate a gospel of effort and self-dependency. And by not taking regular time for biblical self-care, we avoid facing uncomfortable questions such as: Why do I not slow down? What is actually driving me?

Some friends invited my wife and me to join them on a Friday night for a Taize contemplative worship service. The chapel was reverent and quiet. Candles dimly glowed along the walls. The flow of the service was Scripture readings, simple choruses sung over and over, with three periods of silence at different times during the fifty-minute service. The periods of silence were designed to be quiet and listen to the Lord.

The first silence lasted perhaps four minutes. After more singing, the medium silence lasted about seven minutes in length.

I began bracing myself for the "great silence." How could I possibly sit in silence, simply listening for twelve minutes? As the great silence began my mind was struggling — if I could just find a slip of paper and a pen, I could write down some items to place on my to-do list. Or if I could reach my cell phone I could place it on mute and send some text messages. Through the first nine or ten minutes of the great silence I was restless, not resting. I wanted to get something done rather than sit doing nothing for twelve minutes. About Minute 11 into the great silence the Lord's Spirit impressed a simple realization onto my heart. It was as if gently the Spirit was conveying to me, "Paul, you are so busy doing and doing, taking charge of making things happen, that you are not allowing ME to make it happen. It is as if we are on a phone call but you Paul are doing all the talking so I cannot get a word in. When I try to communicate to you, it is as if I always get a busy signal."

There it was: A meaningful mini-Sabbath rest through a twelve-minute silence! I left the service at peace. That is the value of having a rhythm of Sabbaths. Sabbath is worship, which gets our eyes off of ourselves, and in doing so it is also a means of biblical self-care.

"Busyness," even if done for the Lord, can be a symptom of dysfunction, rather than godliness. Any "holic" — whether work-a-holic, alco-holic, ministry-holic — is an indication that our identity — our meaning and well-being — are tied to something other than the Lord Himself. That is the definition of idolatry.

During one Advent season I had become worn out planning and leading our congregation into a meaningful Christmas season. If I could just get through the Christmas Eve service I would finally be off duty for a few days. The service concluded with the lighting of candles. Sarah (the worship leader) and I would each light our candles from the main candle on the communion table. We would each then light the candle of the person on the right or left seat of the center aisle. As light from the candles slowly brightened and snaked its way through the sanctuary, we would all sing Silent Night. It would be a lovely moment.

As Sarah and I stepped to the main candle to light our candles, mine would not light. I thought, *"Come on Lord. This is not funny. I just want to light my candle and get this service over so I can go home."* Sarah sensed my frustration and kindly exchanged candles with me, saying *"Here you take mine."* I lit the candle Sarah gave to me and left her to deal with my rebellious candle. Turning to face the congregation I began lighting the candles of those sitting in the inside seats on one side of the center aisle. I had not passed the second row when I saw Sarah next to me with my rebellious candle blazing like the Olympic torch. Leaning over she whispered, *"You were lighting the wrong end."* Perhaps you have been lighting the wrong end by not having a Sabbath rhythm in your life.

What helps you to stop and rest in the Lord? For me it is unplugging and being in nature. I "sabbath" best when I literally turn off all electronics for the day. No cell phone, no iPad, no computer, no television. Instead I get out walking or hiking in God's creation. It slows me down. It helps me realize in the good sense how small I am and how big the Lord is. I experience the "rest" Jesus promised in Matthew 11:28-30. The word he used for rest is the Greek word meaning rejuvenation, a second wind.

Years ago I was desperately in need of a regular Sabbath. I always have been fascinated by birds of prey – hawks, owls, eagles, and falcons. I began volunteering at a raptor rehabilitation clinic here in Minneapolis. It was a renewing experience for me weekly to fly these gorgeous, wild birds of prey. I did it, rain or shine, for years! They even awarded me with "Volunteer of the Year" recognition.

Do you have hobbies that have nothing to do with Christian work? Typically we are the "experts" others are looking to as the leader. There is an awkward yet satisfying feeling when we are the novice in need of someone else to be our teacher. Over the last several years I took up the banjo – what a joyful, and helpless, dependent feeling. I am at a basic, beginner's level. I NEED a teacher. I also have begun to listen to language CD's, as I try to improve my ability to speak Hebrew.

The same principles of biblical self-care apply to ministries. Is your church or ministry always busy without time for resting and listening to the Lord? As leaders do you have a rhythm of days of listening prayer and retreats?

In an intentional interim pastorate I served, every three months we replaced the normal Sunday service and instead engaged in a concert of prayer as a congregation. It was a tangible way to build a congregational rhythm of turning to the Lord in listening prayer together.

Biblical self-care is not an option. It reboots our hearts, returning us again to the Lord at the center of our lives.

Reflect and Act

I. Are you weary from burning the candle at both ends?

- What is your Sabbath rhythm? How do you practice Sabbath? What will you do?

- Is your life communicating a distorted gospel by being a "-holic"? To what -holic tendencies are you prone?

2. How has this chapter affected your own view and practice of self-care? What will you do?

3. What are we doing, or could we do, to develop a rhythm of Sabbath:

   - Congregationally?

   - As the leadership?

Partner

Share your responses with another leader. Pray together about what stands out to you from your responses.

Dig Deeper

Read Genesis 2:2-3, Psalm 23, Psalm 46:10, Matthew 11:28-30, Mark 1:35, 1 Corinthians 6:19, and 2 Corinthians 6:16.

PERSONALITIES

Chapter 8
Conflict – The Achilles Heel of Ministry

"I know that you believe you understand what you think I said, but I'm not sure you realize that what you heard is not what I meant." Attributed to Robert McCloskey, U.S. State Department spokesman, by Marvin Kalb, CBS News

"Between what I think, what I want to say, what I believe I am saying, what I say, what you want to hear; what you hear; what you believe you understand, what you want to understand, and what you understood, there are at least 9 possibilities for misunderstanding." Francois Garagnon

Most strains and ruptures in ministries are not theological or differences over vision. They are relational. Conflict is inevitable and unavoidable. Conflict is a fork-in-the-road. It is a hands-on opportunity for the Lord to bring personal and inter-personal growth if

> we respond in Christ-pleasing
> rather than God-grieving ways.

After more than thirty-five years in ministry, I am convinced that **_conflict_** is the toughest thing for believers to handle in a Christ-pleasing way.

As Christians we will give of our time and money in sacrificial ways. We will go out of our comfort zones in service efforts, or take steps of faith in life or in prayer. Yet, when it comes to handling our inter-personal conflicts in a Christ-pleasing way, it too rarely happens.

We are not alone. The stories of the Bible are full of conflict – most of which was handled poorly. The first family, Adam and Eve, produced the first homicide, with Cain killing his brother Abel. Abram and Lot separated over an ongoing dispute over land and herds. Jacob and Esau's sibling feud was an extension of the unresolved conflict between their parents, Isaac and Rebekah. Then there is Joseph and his brothers, Moses and Pharaoh (or for that matter, Moses and the Israelites), David and King Saul, or the sad split between the northern and southern kingdoms of Israel. The New Tetament contains more of the same. We see conflict between Jesus and the religious leaders, Jesus and His own disciples, Paul and Barnabas, Paul and Peter, Paul and the Corinthian church, Paul and John Mark, or Eudia and Syntyche noted in Philippians 4:2-3. Conflict is at the root of the the final book in the Bible, Revelation.

My parents were both only children who had difficult up-bringings. My father was raised by a single-parent mother. My mother grew up in an alcoholic family. In their growing-up years, each of my parents had seen unresolved conflict negatively impact them and their families.

As they began their own married life, my parents were determined to have an intact marriage and family.

My parents approach to family conflict was to ignore and avoid it. I can remember times when my mother was upset at the dinner table, and with tears in her eyes would leave the table and lock herself in her bedroom. My father would calmly say to us, *"Your mother is just very tired. She will feel better in the morning."* Somehow we knew that what our dad really meant was to ignore this and in the morning we all will pretend this never happened. I was not equipped to address or constructively resolve conflict. Instead I was raised to be polite, hard-working, and caring and then there would be no conflict.

What a shock it was for me to discover that that was not how things worked in the world of inter-personal relationships. As a newly married twenty-three year old, I recall my wife telling me when she was upset about something. I began to feel tense inside. I did not know what to say or do, and the stress I was feeling made it difficult to breathe. Automatically words came out of my mouth, *"Let's just go to sleep. We will both feel better in the morning."* I was living out what my own parents had modelled – avoid conflict, and it will go away.

Conflict is unavoidable and inevitable

Jesus was perfect, yet His earthly life was filled with conflicts. If Jesus Himself could not avoid conflict, then we are kidding ourselves to think we can live well enough that no one will have a problem with us.

Fresh out of seminary my first church pastorate was serving as the senior pastor of a small church in southern California. In one of my first sermons I stated, *"I am committed to you. This may be the only church I serve."* One of our dear wise seniors pulled me aside and smiling said, *"Paul, you don't want to say that. Paul, love us, lead us, and leave us."* This seemed like strange advice. But as my tenure with that church progressed, I came to understand why he had given me that advice.

Conflict was a habit within the leadership board of that church. One board member noted to me that after board meetings, several board members would go to a local restaurant to conduct a "post mortem on you as the pastor." I was shocked and uncertain what to do about this. Given my upbringing I of course did nothing – avoid conflict, and it will go away. Instead, the problem worsened. Before long it became normal during board meetings that a faction of the board either questioned or directly criticized me. I came to dread board meetings as they approached on the calendar. I would brace myself to get through board meetings. The faction began voicing criticisms of my family during board meetings. As the pastor how should I respond to this from board members?

Marshall Shelley, former editor-in-chief of *Christianity Today* and *Leadership Journal*, noted in his book <u>Well Intentioned Dragons</u> (page 72), *"When attacked by a dragon, do not become one."* I consciously committed not to criticize the critical board members. I chose to pray, asking the Lord to bring resolution and to stop their unloving, unkind behavior.

As the months moved along the situation worsened, as the criticisms continued and became more painful for me. I bit my tongue and poured out my hurt and discouragement to the Lord in prayer, asking Him to bring this to an end. Finally things reached a breaking point. Deeply distressed, I prayed, *"Do something this week to bring it to an end and make it stop, Lord."* He did, but in a most troubling and unexpected way. More about the rest of that story later.

Conflict is a fork in the road. In conflict, relationships will either get better or worse. Trials are both an opportunity for growth, and an opportunity for evil. In James 1:2-12, the word used for "trials" is the same word used for "temptations." A trial is a growth opportunity. A trial is also a temptation. Our response influences whether a trial will be growing pains or painful scars, whether the good God intends or the failing temptation desires is the outcome.

When we mishandle conflict, it grieves God's Spirit, and it bruises and damages the gospel's credibility in the world. When we handle conflict Christ's way, the world takes notice. How can we respond to conflict in God-pleasing ways? And what Spirit-grieving ways do we need to resist during conflicts? What did Jesus intend when He said in Matthew 5:9, "*Blessed are the peacemakers*"?

The entire fifteenth chapter of Luke's gospel is about lost things being found. Jesus is criticized by the religious leaders for spending time with sinners (Luke 15:1-2). In response, Jesus tells three stories, all with the same pattern: something lost, a search until it is found, and a celebration with others to share the joy of lost things being found.

The third and climactic story is about the prodigal son. Actually, it is about both sons and their father. The sons each view life as a report card based on behavior. The youngest son realizes he has failed and made a mess of things and in his remorse gives himself an "F". He rehearses a speech owning his sins, and admitting, "*I am no longer worthy to be called your son.*" (Luke 15:17-19)

In contrast the older brother gives himself an "A". (Luke 15:29) He asserts that he has behaved better than his younger, wayward brother (Luke 15:28-30). The older brother's anger is so intense that he describes his younger sibling not as my brother but as "this son of yours." His anger toward his younger brother is also anger toward his father. He has unresolved conflict with his father and with his younger brother.

Each brother is judging based upon behavior. The younger brother regards himself as a failure because of his wayward behavior. The older brother regards himself as right and his younger sibling (and father) as wrong. Conflict is straining and damaging their family relationships, dividing the brothers from each other and from their father.

In contrast, the father's heart is radically different from his sons'. The father's heart is for restored relationship:

> Quick! Bring the finest robe in the house and put it on him. Get a ring for his finger and sandals for his feet. And kill the calf we have been fattening. We must celebrate with a feast, for this son of mine was dead and has now returned to life. He was lost, but now he is found. (Luke 15:22-24)

So the party began.

That same heart for restored relationship shapes the father's comments to the older angry son:

> His father said to him, "Look, dear son, you have always stayed by me, and everything I have is yours. We had to celebrate this happy day. For your brother was dead and has come back to life! He was lost, but now he is found!" (Luke 15:31-32)

God's desire in conflict is for healing and restoration of relationship, not for a winner and loser. Lost things need to be found and celebrated! Lost people need to be found and celebrated!

From the prodigal son, to the cross of Jesus, the Lord's heart-beat is for restored relationship, rather than keeping track of offenses and deciding who is more right and who is more wrong.

Spirit-grieving reactions to conflict

Paul commanded believers in Ephesus *"do not grieve the Holy Spirit of God".* Translated literally it says - *stop grieving the Holy Spirit.* (Ephesians 4:29-5:2). What are Spirit-grieving reactions during conflict?

Fighting and blaming

Galatians 5:15 soberly warns, *"If you bite and devour each other, watch out or you will be destroyed by each other."*

Not far from my home there is a church located in a desirable outer ring suburb. The church has a lovely facility, in a great location. The church has in excess of one million dollars in reserves. Yet that church was divided by years of fighting between two groups that had solidified in their dislike and distrust of one another. That church closed its doors. The issue was not money – the congregation had a large surplus of funds. The issue was not facility – the church had an appealling building and location. The issue was that the congregants kept biting and devouring one another. The sad pricetag they paid for insisting they were right in their feud was the destruction of the church itself.

When you or I insist on nursing our wounds, insisting that we are right and the other party is wrong, we give evil a toehold (Ephesians 4:27). When we claim God's forgiveness in Christ, and yet refuse to forgive others who have wronged us, we contradict and damage the gospel's credibility. When the watching world sees us fighting, feuding, and blaming, they turn away from considering Christ. That pricetag is too for you or me to indulge in supposedly being right.

Are you, or others you know, grieving the Lord by fighting and blaming?

<u>False peace</u>

"False peace" is ignoring conflict and being dishonest. Have you been in a conflict with another person yet when asked by that person if there was a problem, you denied it saying, *"No, we are fine. Don't worry about it."* We are doing what the people in Jeremiah's day did – healing the wound superficially. Flattery can be dishonest. Denying we have a conflcit to that person's face, while criticizing him or her behind his or her back is dishonest.

> *Like a coating of silver dross on earthenware*
> * are fervent lips with an evil heart.*
> *Enemies disguise themselves with their lips,*
> * but in their hearts they harbor deceit.*
> *Though their speech is charming, do not believe them,*
> * for seven abominations fill their hearts.*
> *Their malice may be concealed by deception,*
> * but their wickedness will be exposed in the assembly.*
> (Proverbs 26:23-26)

Are you, or others you know, grieving the Lord by denying and being dishonest about a conflict?

Gossip

Gossip is passing on information that should not be shared, whether or not true. A senior congregant was visiting with her friends after the worship service. I overheard her voicing criticisms about a staff member. I stopped and said to her, *"It gives me no pleasure to do this but I have to tell you that you are gossiping, and I urge you to stop immediately."* She denied she was gossiping, insisting, *"It is not gossip because what I am saying is true."* She did not understand the meaning of gossip.

Slander is speaking untruths. Gossip is spreading information, true or not, to others who did not need to know that information.

I like chocolate chip cookie dough. Why wait to cook it when you can scoop thick, sugary batter out of the bowl, with tasty morsels of chocolate chips in each delicious spoonful? Gossip is juicy, tasty news about others. It tastes good. It is hard to resist. We want another scoop. Proverbs 26:22 describes the appeal of gossip, *"The words of a gossip are like choice morsels; they go down to the inmost parts."*

But gossip is destructive, damaging relationships. _The Message_ version of Proverbs 16:28 reads, *"Gossips break up friendships."* Proverbs 6:16-19 is a fire alarm alerting us of six things the Lord hates, seven that are an abomination to Him. The final, seventh thing the Lord hates is *"a person who stirs up conflict in the community."*

Are you, or others you know, grieving the Lord by gossiping, passing on information that should be left private?

Spend a few moments checking yourself for any God-grieving attitudes or actions in your relationships.

God-pleasing responses in conflict

What are God-pleasing ways to respond to conflict in our lives? How can we be in step with God's heart for restoration, rather than be "winners" and "losers"?

Don't get started

How I could possibly come up with an entire sermon based upon a simple statement no longer than a fortune cookie.? But my first seminary preaching assignment was just one verse, Proverbs 17:14. I read it, and then I read the verse again, and again, and again. Soon I was wondering how I would be able to fit everything it had to say into a single sermon. Proverbs 17:14 says, "*Starting a quarrel is like breaching a dam; so drop the matter before the dispute breaks out.*"

Like an infected wound, or a cracked dam, a conflict can burst open, spilling into the lives of innocent bystanders. In other words, in unresolved conflict, other people can become co-lateral damage.

In a conflict where you have been offended or misunderstood, can you overlook it and let it go? If so, then "drop the matter." Romans 14:1 speaks of not *"quarreling over disputable matters"*.

One of my dear friends is also a mentor role model for me. Occasionally we have disagreed on an issue. Often he calmly will say with a kind expression, "*I want to disagree without being disagreeable.*" There it is, a tangible way to "drop the matter" and not engage in arguing over disputable matters.

Can you, or others you are helping, please God by dropping a quarrel before it breaks out?

Self-examination

Remember the story I shared about the first church and the critical faction of the board? Here is the rest of the story.

I had prayed, urging the Lord to "bring it to an end this week". As I prayed I sensed the Spirit asking me a simple question: *"Paul, what is your heart attitude toward those men?"* My immediate response was self-defense as I said, *"I have not retaliated or behaved like them."* The Lord's Spirit persisted with His same question, *"But what is your heart attitude toward them?"* I expressed that I did not hate them, but realized that was far short of the command of Jesus to love others. Convicted, I honestly admitted my attitude was not one of love toward those men. I knew the Lord was prompting me to confess my lack of love to those men who had wronged me. This was not fair! I was not the one who started this conflict. And I had resisted spreading it to others or retaliating in criticism.

For three days I struggled with the Lord. If this was how he treats those He calls into vocational ministry, then I will leave ministry and do something different – for more money and less pain and humility. But I could not escape the conviction that I was to bring the board together and confess my shortcoming to them. I phoned the chairman, asking him to convence a special meeting of the board. As hard as it was to do, I knew I was doing what would please the Lord.

I felt at peace as I headed to the meeting. After the seven board members had gathered, I shared openly and honestly my confession that I had fallen short in Christ's command to love them. I added, *"I am not saying all of our problems are my fault, but the Lord has convicted me that I need to take responsibility for my part and I'm doing that now."* The first reaction was from one of the critical board members, who said, *"What are you trying to pull here?"* For a brief moment I was tempted to say to the Lord – *"Do you see? I knew they would use this against me."* Instead, I simply said, *"I have done what I felt led by the Lord to do. We can go home if that is what you want to do now."* Another board member spoke up, challenging us each to speak aloud and "own" our heart attitudes. As man after man spoke, it was obvious they together agreed that as a leadership board we were stinking up the church. The sharing was like lancing a puss-infected wound.

Jesus said in Matthew 7:5, *"You hypocrite, first take the plank out of your own eye, and then you will see clearly to remove the speck from your brother's eye."* In other words, if you cannot overlook an offense, then the next step is self-examination. In *Resolving Everyday Conflict*, the organization Peacemakers puts it this way: Even if you think you are only responsible for 2% of a conflict, you should take 100% responsibility for that 2%.

One of my trusted and wise friends listened patiently as I complained about criticisms being directed at me as a pastor. After quietly listening, my friend said to me, *"Does the shoe fit?"* My friend was helping by challenging me to look in the mirror and do self-examination.

Do you need to look in the mirror and examine your heart attitdues and actions as a next God- pleasing step in your conflict?

Keep the circle as small as possible

Maintain privacy. Jesus advised His followers in Matthew 18:15, *"If your brother or sister sins, go and point out their fault, just be-tween the two of you. If they listen to you, you have won them over."* The *New Living Translation* uses the phrase "go privately." In resolving wrongs, keep the circle as small as possible.

Does your heart desire what God's heart desires – restoration and healing of the relationship? Go privately to that person with whom you have a conflict. Be honest (Proverbs 27:6), but speak truth in love (Ephesians 4:15).

I have found *The Message* translation of James 1:19-20 has often been a helpful reminder for me, *"Lead with your ears, follow up with your tongue, and let anger straggle along in the rear. God's righteousness doesn't grow from human anger."* Lead wiith your ears. Listen well. Listen long. Listen to understand. Aim for understanding the other person's perspective and feelings. The simple phrase "help me understand," followed by patient listening, can contribute to healing a conflict.

Do you need to keep the circle small, going privately as a next God-pleasing step in your conflict?

Get "helpful help"

Get "helpful help" if you can't resolve your conflict privately. Euodia and Sytyche are preserved for us in Chapter four of Paul's letter to the Philippians. Active in the cause of Christ, these two women could not resolve their differences with each other. Paul asked for outside help, *"I ask you, my true companion, help these women since they have contended at my side in the cause of the gospel."* (Philippians 4:2-3)

If you are unable to resolve your conflict privately, alone between you and the person with whom you are at odds, then get helpful help. Matthew 18:16-20 speaks of involving two or three witnesses. Jesus does not mean recruit your friends to join you in ganging up on the person with whom you have a conflict. He is referring to a passage in Deuteronomy about settling disputes by enlisting mature, fair-minded persons who can mediate and render a fair solution. (Deuteronomy 19:14-18) When you involve others, make sure whenever possible that the two or three witnesses are acceptable and credible to both parties in the conflict. That will increase the chances of a resolution leading to restoration.

Matthew 18 lays out an additional step of informing the entire church, or likely the leadership of the church community. This is not a requirement, but rather an option. This step is more formal, and can lead to expulsion from the church community. (Matthew 18:17) Jesus says if a conflict is unresolved, and if one party *"refuses to listen,"* the leaders can *"treat that person as a pagan or a corrupt tax collector."* In other words, that party's behavior in the conflict is not that of a Christ-follower, so treat that person as someone who does not have faith in Christ – as a Gentile or tax gatherer. That does not mean the person should be shunned or shamed. Instead, it means that person should be viewed as am unbeliever, reaching out to him or her as someone who does not yet follow Christ.

In ministry I have occasionally been in conflicts with others. In some of those conflicts I found the person unwilling to resolve the conflict. I faced a judgment call – do I make this a formal process, bringing it to the leadership, or do I let it go? While I had the right to make it a formal issue, I had to consider if that would be helpful.

The entire focus of Matthew 18 is about forgiveness and re-storing relationship. (See Matthew 18:21-35). As discussed in Chapter 2, it is about the Vertical (how the Lord treats us) becoming the Horizontal (how we treat others). Each step in God-pleasing conflict resolution needs to be taken with that spirit and goal.

What if you cannot resolve the conflict with the other person?

Years ago a very good friend lost respect for me and left the church, even sending an open letter to the church body stating it. It was deeply painful and also publicly embarassing to me. I contacted him, asking if we could meet to address and resolve whatever had offended him. We set a lunch meeting, which he then cancelled. We set another lunch meeting, which he again cancelled. I made seven contacts with him seeking to meet in person. Each time he delayed or declined. I realized that he was unwilling to meet with me. What is our responsibility if due to the other person's unwillingness, we are unable to resolve a conflict? Romans 12:18 helped me, "*As much as it depends on you, be at peace with all men.*"

I had done all I could to be at peace with my friend. I sent him a letter noting that I had tried seven times to meet, and he clearly was not yet interested in meeting with me. I let him know that I would no longer pursue him, but that I would be ready and willing to resolve our conflict whenever he felt ready to do so. I left the next move up to him.

Eighteen years later we were sitting together over lunch. We talked over the eighteen years of no communication. We were honest. We reconciled. Toward the end of our visit, as the bill arrived, he insisted on paying for the lunch. I suggested we split the bill. Instead my friend said, "*Let me pay this time, Paul, and you can pay the next time.*" And six weeks later, we had a second enjoyable lunch together. During those eighteen years I prayed for him and his family. I did not speak negatively about him. Happily, the Lord allowed us to finally address our conflict and restore our friendship. But during those eighteen years, Romans 12:18 enabled me to be at peace, even though the conflict had not yet been resolved.

Have you done all you can to live at peace with the person with whom you are in conflict? Are there any further God-pleasing steps you can take, or is it time to get on with your life?

Grow from the pain

Conflicts are a fork-in-the-road. Conflict with others is un-voidable and inevitable. As my colleague Gregg Caruso puts it, conflicts can be a *"grace disguised growth opportunity."* In your conflicts, don't waste the pain. Use Appendix C as a guide that provides a short listing of God-grieving vs. God-pleasing responses to conflict.

Many people are like the walking wounded from past conflicts. Rather than gaining from the pain, they have become fragile, fearful, defensive, bitter, or unwilling to face and work through conflict. When we react in Spirit-grieving ways, we lose personally, and the gospel loses credibility.

As followers of Christ, we can respond in God-pleasing ways to conflict and gain growth in our own lives, while becoming a living illustration of the power of the gospel.

Reflect and Act

1. How was conflict handled in the family in which you grew up? What was modeled for you?

   • What was helpful, consistent with God-pleasing ways of resolving conflict?

   • What was unhelpful, Spirit-grieving ways of not resolving conflict?

2. Think of a current (or recent) conflict in which you are:

    • Is your heart desire for lost things to be found and restored, or is your heart wanting to see the other person suffer?

    • How can the Vertical (how Jesus treats you) become the Horizontal (how you treat others) in your conflict? What specific attitudes or actions might you change?

3. Review the specifics about Spirit-grieving and God-pleasing responses to conflict in this Chapter (and summarized in Appendix C).

    • Are there any Spirit-grieving attitudes or behaviors from which you need to break free?

    • Are there any God-pleasing steps on which you need to act?

4. Do you know others who are struggling with a conflict right now? How can you help them to respond in God-pleasing, rather than Spirit-grieving, ways?

Partner

Share your responses with another leader. Pray together about what stands out to you from your responses.

Dig Deeper

Read Matthew 5:9, Matthew 18, Romans 12:18, Ephesians 4:30-5:2, and James 1:2-5, 4:1-10.

PERSONALITIES

Chapter 9
Building Teams

"If one of us would just get off, I could have a lot more fun." A Kindergartener fighting with a classmate over a tricycle

"Volunteers have to get more satisfaction from their work than paid employees, precisely because they do not get a paycheck." Peter Drucker, _Management's New Paradigms_

Healthy leadership teams do not happen easily or by accident. How do you build healthy teams? The _Boys In The Boat : Nine Americans and Their Epic Quest for Gold at the 1936 Berlin Olympics_, by Daniel James Brown, tells the story of the rowing team from the University of Washington.

"In rowing parlance, swing is that quality associated with a boat that is working in unison." It's not hard work when the rhythm comes – that "swing" as they call it. I've heard men shriek out with delight when that swing came in an eight; it's a thing they'll never forget as long as they live." George Yeoman Pocock

How can a team find its swing? We all are acquainted with I Corinthians 12, the chapter about the body of Christ. We know it, but do we really live it out? When friction and conflict breaks out within a leadership team, it is too late to do team-building.

Driving to my first day as the interim pastor of a new church, I received a cell phone call from one of the pastoral staff. With enthusiasm he said to me, "*Hey, the pastoral staff was thinking it would be fun to meet off-site to grab lunch together and then play Frisbee golf for a few hours.*"

I could not believe it – did they actually expect me to spend my first official day out of the office? What would the receptionist say to people who phoned to talk to me, "No, I'm sorry. Pastor Paul won't be in today. He is out playing Frisbee golf with the rest of the pastors." Every instinct inside me wanted to say "no," and then I caught myself. Why did staff want to play Frisbee golf with me? If this was their idea, did I really want to start my relationships with them by saying "no"? I agreed to the lunch and Frisbee golf.

It turned out to be a brilliant suggestion. We bonded as a staff team more in an afternoon of Frisbee golf than we would have in months of meetings. We laughed, we had fun, and we got to know each other as people. Each individual personality surfaced as we chatted and joked during Frisbee golf. By the end of that afternoon my relationships with the staff pastors had taken a large leap forward. That church became the most enjoyable of all the churches I have served in terms of staff morale.

Teenagers cannot receive a driver's license without first having a learner's permit. In many states engaged couples receive a discount on the cost of a marriage license if they complete 12 hours of pre-marital counseling. Yet in Christian ministries we assume that leadership teams will function smoothly without any training.

The strongest team I was a part of was a faith-based non-profit serving at-risk teens. There were four of us on the senior leadership team. Each of us was quite different. Imagine the four of us having a picnic on the edge of a tall, steep cliff. The founder was a true entrepreneur who had visions. He was a risk-taker. He would run full speed, leaping off the edge of the cliff, shouting to all of us, "*Come on, jump! God is going to do something amazing.*" By nature I prefer new things more than maintenance. I like leaping, but not recklessly. I would attach a bungee cord to my leg and then leap off the cliff saying, "*Why not?*" The third member of our team would keenly watch who had leaped off the cliff. He would cup his hands to his mouth and shout, "*I want you both to know that I believe in taking leaps of faith, and I support your risk-taking spirit. I may be joining you, but first I need to do some research about the wind speed, what is at the bottom of the canyon, and how close by the nearest medical center is from here. Once I gather that information, then I will get back to you about if I am willing to jump.*" The fourth member of our team would be sliding back as far away from the cliff as possible, while shouting to us, "*Is there anything I can do to make your fall more comfortable?*"

We were four very different personalities, yet we became a highly united and productive team. It did not happen naturally.

We worked at it. We worked at our relationships. We spent lots of time listening to each other's opinions and feelings. We were committed to the mission, not our egos. We had conflicts. We each brought humble, servant spirits rather than attitudes of power and control. Over time we learned to highly value and respect each other. We knew that any decision would be better if it passed through the full team, even though that could be tiring and at times tried our patience.

Any organization will not mature beyond the maturity of its leadership. Practically, how do you become a highly functioning team? Alignment of purpose, culture, and roles produces that "swing" of a highly functioning team.

> **Any organization will not mature beyond the maturity of its leadership.**

Purpose

In the absence of a clear and commonly-shared vision, most people focus on their program. The result is siloed staff and segmented people passionate about a specific program. Program (what we are doing) becomes the focus, rather than purpose (why we are here). When a team is not united around a common purpose, people tend to defend their program, citing how much good it has accomplished. Staff resists change and defends their time — insisting they are so busy keeping existing programs going that they cannot take on anything new. Key volunteers and staff become turf-defenders. Program, rather than purpose, becomes the emotional focus.

A written statement of purpose may or may not be the actual, real purpose. The actual purpose is what really drives people to give and serve, and shapes what they talk about and what stories they share. The actual purpose is whatever you are determined to do, or die trying. What is it you are determined to do, or die trying? For those in Christian ministry, our purpose must center on moving people God-ward.

> **Your actual purpose is whatever you are determined to do, or die trying.**

I frequently am asked to help churches clarify their purpose and then align their entire ministry around that purpose. Each church has its own particular way of describing its central vision, its purpose. Common to each church's purpose is an upward focus (relationship with God), an inward focus (relationships within the body of believers) and an outward focus (relationships with the community and the world around us). The members of one church translated their purpose into a congregational hand motion – lifting their arms "upward," then bringing their arms waist high and moving them around as a circle, and then extending their arms outward. As the members made that simple 3-step hand motion, they together said, "Upward, inward, and outward." It became a tangible way to remind everyone of their purpose.

Culture

Purpose should shape the culture of the organization. Organizations develop a DNA that becomes their culture. More than simply how work is done, the culture is the environment – the emotional and relational reality of that organization – in which work is done. In underperforming, unhealthy organizations, the culture itself reinforces poor health. I work with churches in crisis or transition. They have reached the point of knowing they cannot go on as they have been living. Part of restoring health often means changing the culture.

During a half-day retreat with staff, I asked them, "*What do you want to characterize our working environment? What kind of workplace do you want to work in such that you will commit to fostering each other?*" We spent time discussing and deciding what we would do to make the culture, our working environment. We committed to live and lovingly hold one another accountable to create that culture. In some cases this meant confronting and resolving baggage from the past, such as distrust and disrespect that had soured staff relationships.

When asked what kind of culture do you want to work in and commit to foster, here are the four words chosen by staff:

- TRUST – turning to the Lord will be our first and regular reflex; it is good to always have to trust Him rather than feel we have everything under control

- TEAM – you are not alone, we are in this together; your success is our success, your problems are our problems; pull your weight; be honest; live a balanced life; have fun

- TALENT – training and giving constructive feedback to staff, and tapping talent in the body

- TRAJECTORY – our agreed-upon purpose is the tail that wags the dog, including our roles and what stories we highlight

We took those four words that most described our desired culture – Trust, Team, Talent, Trajectory – and painted them onto four signs. They hang in the church office as visible reminders to ourselves.

Roles

As purpose and culture are clarified, the next step in team-building is aligning roles. In view of the central purpose for which we are determined to do or die trying to see happen, what key roles and volunteer teams are needed? This can include reviewing and potentially revising job descriptions, while being honest about job fit. It may also mean reviewing and revising or creating volunteer teams necessary to make progress on the church's purpose. Be clear and realistic about expectations, and provide constructive, candid feedback. This applies both to staff and volunteer teams.

Utilize people in their strength areas. What if Moses had dismissed his father-in-law's advice as "old school ideas from an old man"? By paying attention to Jethro's administrative advice, Moses' own role became more manageable. Nehemiah was a visionary leader spearheading a capital rebuilding effort. Yet beginning in Nehemiah chapter 8, it is Ezra who surfaces and leads a spiritual renewal. Rather than being threatened or engaging in a power struggle with Ezra, Nehemiah welcomed Ezra to use gifts that were different from his own. The result was that rebuilding the wall became the springboard for the spiritual renewal of God's people.

Remember that synergistic team of four I mentioned earlier in this chapter? Once each year we devoted a day together reviewing our strategic vision and plan. For each of the previous five years, one strategic goal was to train others in using our model of ministry with at-risk teens. We believed that our model of ministry was transferable, that it would work in different settings. But each year there was no action. For five straight years it remained a written strategic goal that each year was affirmed and then tabled with no action.

In my frustration I spoke up, recommending that we delete it, since for five straight years we had done nothing to act on it. A lively debate followed, lasting about forty-five minutes. The outcome was that the leadership team wanted to see that strategic goal happen, but we lacked a driver, a point person who would own and lead the effort.

I spoke again saying, *"Good news, our problem is solved – I will do it. Give that assignment to me. I would love to lead that charge."* Some on the team were surprised. They had come to view me only in my current role. They had forgotten to pay attention to people's skills and passions. I had to help them see that I had other skills that were not being utilized but matched a key strategic goal for which we needed a leader. They agreed to let me lead that initiative.

Over the next few years we saw significant action and lasting progress in training others to use our ministry model with at-risk youth. I had the satisfaction of using some of my talents, while we saw growth in the ministry.

How are you giving time and attention to team-building? Team-building rarely happens spontaneously. It is difficult for team-building relationships to occur in agenda-driven meeting. Do you understand who are the introverts and the extroverts on the team and what the implications are for your meetings? Who are the big-picture vs. nuts-and-bolts, practical people? Which people think relationally, and which think logically? Who on the team is wired to stick to decisions made, and who is open to flexing as new information comes to light? Who has gifts of the "head," the "heart," or the "hands"? How can the team tap each person's different gifts when they are needed?

Make team-building an ongoing priority among staff and key volunteers. There are many resources available to help in team-building, such as LifeKeys, StrengthsFinder, Meyers-Briggs, Shape, and others.

Beyond sharing and learning about one another, follow up with action. Live out what you learn about one another to change how your team interacts with one another. Let action cause you to tap into the different talents on your team or modify someone's role to allow him or her to major on his or her skills and passions.

Team-building is hard work because people are different. If you overlook ongoing team-building, the health and productivity of the team and the ministry will suffer. The good news is that when we invest in growing healthy leadership teams, our investment produces Christ-honoring results in us as leaders and in the ministry.

Reflect and Act

1. What is your purpose? What are you so determined about that you will do it or die trying?

2. What is your ministry's purpose? What is it determined to do or die trying?

3. In what ways have programs become more important than purpose in your ministry? Siloing is one indication that programs are more important than purpose.

4. For what would you most like the culture, your working environment, to be known?

    •   Which of those traits is already part of the culture?

- What traits, if any, need to be challenged and changed in the culture?

5. Do you know the talents on your team? Are they being maximized?

   - Is your role a good fit for your talents and interests? How so? How not?

   - What are the talents of others on your team? Do their roles allow them to major on their skills and talents?

   - How are you (or could you) consciously identify and utilize the different gifts and experiences of those on your team?

   - Are there any talents missing that need to be added to your team?

Partner

Share your responses with another leader. Pray together about what stands out to you from your responses.

Dig Deeper

Read John 17, 1 Corinthians 12-13, and 1 Timothy 3:10-11.

PRACTICE

Chapter 10
Boards as Overseers

"I'm their leader, which way did they go?", printed on a baseball cap with two bills

"Care for the flock that God has entrusted to you. Watch over it willingly, not grudgingly — not for what you will get out of it, but because you are eager to serve God. Don't lord it over the people assigned to your care, but lead them by your own good example." I Peter 5:2-3

Biblical leaders are mature people who have been shaped by life experience to firmly trust and follow God, His purpose, and His ways. They become point people who verbalize, mobilize, and organize people-movement God-ward so that people come to know and grow in Christ.

What does it mean and not mean to be overseers of God's flock? Literally, "overseer" means to see over, to watch over. For example, when my children were in school and had homework, it was my responsibility to see that they got their homework done. It was not my responsibility to do their homework for them. As a teenager my son did his homework with music playing, plus two computer screens lit up in front of him. I would not have been able to concentrate with those multi-media distractions. Yet he was getting his homework done and getting decent grades. I was seeing over him, getting the homework done, while giving him freedom to determine how he got it done. It had to get done – that was my oversight role. How it got done was up to him.

Leaders, whether called elders, council members, directors, pastors, or sessions, must be mature spiritually and in life experience. The New Testament emphasizes character and maturity as essential for any leader of God's family. My distillation of I Timothy 3 is that a leader must be a person of integrity, in other words, a person with an integrated life. Another way of saying this is that leaders are to be consistent – who I am at work is who I am at home and at church. That consistency will be seen in lifestyle, attitudes, and relationships.

Purposeful relationships

God's family is about purposeful relationships. More than just relationships, as Christ's followers we are called to special, purposeful relationship – with the Lord, and with others. In John 17 Jesus prayed for purposeful relationships among his followers.

Paul spoke of this in Philippians 1:27, "*Whatever happens, conduct yourselves in a manner worthy of the gospel of Christ. Then, whether I come and see you or only hear about you in my absence, I will know that you stand firm in the one Spirit, striving together as one for the faith of the gospel.*" He returns to this emphasis on purposeful relationship in the next chapter, "*Make my joy complete by being like-minded, having the same love, being one in spirit and of one mind."* (Philippians 2:2)

Biblical leaders are mature people who have been shaped by life experience to firmly trust and follow God, His purpose, and His ways. They become point people who verbalize, mobilize, and organize people-movement God-ward so that people come to know and grow in Christ.

In other words, as overseers, keep your eye on the ball – which is Jesus and living out His Great Commandment and Great Commission. As leaders we are responsible to see over the body getting that homework done. Measure health and progress against those two commands – are God's people growing in how they love Him and in how they love others, which includes reaching not-yet-believers with the life-changing gospel of Christ?

As Andy Stanley noted in <u>Deep and Wide</u>, *"Marry your mission. Date your model. Fall in love with your vision. Stay mildly infatuated by your approach."* Keep ministry aligned with Jesus' purpose. Track progress, highlight those stories, celebrate those successes, and expect staff to major on programming that accomplishes Jesus' great commandment and great commission purpose. How they choose to get it done (programs) can be left to them, but as overseers we are responsible to keep God's flock focused on living out His purpose. Lovingly and honestly see that evaluation of programs is happening. Celebrate progress, make adjustments, eliminate unproductive or rogue programs, and risk by trying new steps that might further the purpose of Jesus.

Make constructive evaluation of staff and programs a normal expectation. Otherwise programs can replace purpose, and keeping a program going becomes the purpose in itself. Activity is not the same as productivity in ministry.

Example

We are to be examples. Is your own life a good model of relying on the Spirit as you major on living out the Great Commandment and the Great Commission? As leaders do we pray for and lovingly hold one another accountable to be examples of those commands showing up in our own lives?

People respond to and follow leaders who are living examples. Time and again I have seen troubled, fractured, angry churches begin to move toward health as the leaders lived out humility and transparency. When leadership is healthy and growing, the church will sense it and follow. Beyond simply making decisions and reviewing operations, what are we doing as leaders so that we ourselves are growing as disciples? Is training time part of the leadership experience in your church? Have you grown and matured in prayer, evangelism, compassion, forgiveness, faith, generosity, humility, etc. from being part of leadership in your ministry?

Part of being overseers of God's flock means we devote time to work on our own growth individually and as a team. Become the change you want to see. As Paul urged in 1 Timothy 4:15, *"Be diligent in these matters; give yourself wholly to them, so that everyone may see your progress."* I find that a devotional time at the start of a leadership meeting is nice, but it usually has a short shelf-life. By the time the leadership meeting ends, most people have a hard time recalling the topic of the devotional. I still offer a devotional and time of prayer at the beginning or end of a leadership meeting. I also schedule extended time for training with the leadership team. Two meetings per month is a realistic rhythm. One meeting focuses on the leadership items of overseeing the ministry, such as finances, ministry updates, policies, motions, etc. The second meeting of the month focuses on shepherding people, such as those needing care, correction, or development. This second meeting includes a training time and an extended prayer time. It is a non-business meeting.

> **Become the change you want to see.**

Teamwork between the key leader and the board

What is a productive working relationship between the governing board and the pastor or key leader? Frequently this is an area of confusion and frustration. Each has assumptions what the working relationship should be, however, often they have not come to a common understanding and practice. Is the pastor the leader, the first among equals, or an employee? To whom is the board accountable?

Like a healthy marriage or a successful sports team, the board and pastor must work together as a team, while living their distinct and different roles. It is a relationship of working "with" one another, not a hierarchy of one working "for" the other. Like a sport team with an offense and a defense, both need each other to succeed. If an offense scores 20 points per game but the defense gives up 24 points per game, the team does not win. In healthy ministries there is a clear effective working relationship between the board and the key leader.

The board is not called to be supportive or unsupportive of the pastor. Rather, the board is to effectively team with the pastor in overseeing the well-being and progress of the ministry. The board is accountable to the Lord for staying on "mission" and for overseeing the well-being and maturing of the body. The pastor has authority to programmatically lead and carry out the church's mission, including supervising staff. The board is to stay out of management matters, such as supervision of staff or program issues. The board exercises accountability with the lead pastor through an annual performance evaluation.

Common clarity and agreement among the governing board about what their roles are, and are not, is vital. Without common agreement the governing board will be at the whim of the current opinions of those on the board. Appendix D provides a sample board manual outline developed by one of the churches I had the joy of working with as an interim pastor. The church was in an emotional crisis over the departure of its pastor. The leadership board was unclear about where their role began and ended. Staff felt disempowered and discouraged. There was distrust of pastors and, for some, a distrust of the board. We devoted time to clarifying the role of the board, the role of the pastor, and the role of staff. After several months they came to agreement on what a healthy working relationship could look like between the board and pastor.

Recovering trust started with transparent communication – among the board members themselves, between the board and staff, and between the board and the congregation. Transparent communication was not merely informational; it also had to be relational – confessing failings, acknowledging ignorance, expressing feelings of hurt, distrust, and resentment. Along with improved communication we clarified the roles of board, pastor, and staff. Living out those new clarified roles, and catching one another when we slipped into old bad habits helped strengthen hope and trust. As we made progress living out new clarified roles in a spirit of humility and teamwork, the morale of leadership and the entire church improved.

Another board I worked with was functionally dysfunctional. The absence of clarity or agreement about the role of the board was producing frustration, exhaustion, and lack of significant results. A return to health and productivity began when we honestly acknowledged the dysfunction. We revisited the biblical role to oversee, not to manage. We clarified the roles of the board, the lead pastor, the pastoral staff, and the congregation, laying it out visually in a simple Responsible-Accountable-Consulted-Informed (RACI) chart. It gave us clarity about each one's lanes, and allowed us to function more effectively — to ask questions when someone was uncertain about his or her role, and to exercise accountability when someone veered out of his or her role.

Relationships

Most ministries break down over relationship, not over doctrine, vision, or program issues. Healthy interpersonal relationships among the leadership are crucial. Jesus' new command to *"love one another as I have loved you"* (repeated in John 15;11-12, 15:17, I Corinthians 13, Ephesians 5:1-2, Galatians 5:6, 5:22-23; I Timothy 1:5, and I John) is foundational. To fall short of or ignore Jesus' command risks morphing church into a business, rather than being the body of Christ. Board members must model healthy relationships. This inevitably will include biblical peacemaking of conflicts, aiming for understanding and restoration, rather than judging right and wrong. As leaders, are you balancing "grace and truth" like Jesus (John 1:14)? How are you living out Peter's call to clothe yourselves with humility toward one another (I Peter 5:5)? As leaders, are you placing the well-being of the body over the rights, preferences, or complaints of any individual?

Communication

Communication is a major challenge in churches and minis-tries. Attenders and members span different backgrounds, different ages, generations, and stages of life, and different ways of learning and retaining information. People appreciate and trust leadership that communicates. Are you making it easy for people to know what is going on within the life of the ministry? Use multiple channels of communication – ver-bal announcements, printed updates, websites, group emails, smart phone apps, face-to-face forums, home meetings, etc.

Leaders sometimes assume that because they are the leaders, they can simply make decisions and declare those decisions. This may be true on paper, but emotions shape how people hear and react to information.

When trust levels are high, leadership can lead, and the body will normally respond and follow. When trust levels are mixed or low, leadership needs to pay attention to the emotional and relational dynamics within the body. During anxious times leadership should increase transparent communication, includ-ing two-way communication that allows people to be heard.

More than once I have worked with a church reeling from emotional and relational fallout after a major decision by leadership. One church was struggling with its pastor. Some wanted the pastor to stay, while others felt it was time for a change. Grumbling and defending, gossip and criticisms, and prolonged debates among the governing board were the norm over many months. Ultimately it came to a congregational vote whether to retain or terminate the pastor. The vote was 52% to 48%. Clearly the church was divided. Some who voted for the pastor to be terminated left the church. Attendance and giving declined. A few months later the pastor opted to resign.

112

I arrived as the intentional interim pastor to a fractured, hurting, divided congregation. Several months into my tenure during an adult gathering, one leader mentioned the vote to terminate the pastor. He commented, "*It was a simple question. People either voted for or against removing the pastor.*" But what appeared simple to him was not so simple. An individual expressed, "*That pastor conducted my father's funeral. I was not about to vote to terminate him.*" Another person observed, "*The family had medical needs, and if I voted to terminate him, they would not have health insurance.*" The leaders assumed it was a simple, straightforward decision, yet others saw that decision through a variety of emotional and relational lenses.

To help churches recover trust and unity, I developed the Church Check-Up. It is a participatory process that engages the entire church body. It results in a clear picture of the church's health, while increasing unity and providing a clarified direction for the church's next steps. For a sample summary report from a church that used the Church Check-Up, see Appendix E. Similar to going to your doctor for an annual physical exam, the Church Check-Up has brought healing, clarity, and rejuvenated focus and energy in many churches that were stuck or struggling with issues of trust and direction.

Faith not force

As overseers, we are responsible but not powerful enough to make others live out the mission of Jesus. That is the work of God's Spirit. As leaders how are we flexing our faith muscles by relying on the Spirit to work in people's hearts? Faith moves people more than force. Trust moves people more than control. Prayer moves people more than policies. I wish every church had a person like my friend Ted. He has made prayer a reflex. When someone shares with Ted a concern or a need, he listens attentively and then says, "*Father, we are asking you to meet this need in Paul's life."* He does not promise to pray for you, he pauses and prays right then and there for you. He is an example of living out trust in the Spirit's power through prayer. How much is Spirit-dependent prayer woven into our work as leaders? Consider making 2 Corinthians 3:3, 3:18, and 4:7 a regular part of your praying together as leaders.

Leading is important. Effective leading by boards means we as leaders are examples of what we want others to value. It requires that as a leadership team we are clear on our role, that we actively work at preserving healthy relationships among our team, and that we have transparent communication with people. And as leaders our focus and confidence for moving people needs to continually be seen in faith in the Lord, rather than using force.

Reflect and Act

1. Are the roles (what is and is not the responsibility of your governing board members) known and lived out by board members?

2. Are there any areas of confusion or frustration in leadership responsibilities that need to be addressed and resolved? Be specific.

   • Role of our key leader

   • Role of the board

3. As you reflect on your current leadership team, on a scale of 1 to 5 (with 1 being poor, and 5 being excellent), how would you rate the group on:

   • Oversight vs. management?

- Being living examples of the key priorities of the ministry?

- Healthy relationships among board members, including conflict resolution?

- Productive time given to team-building and training of the board?

- Spirit-dependent prayer?

- Communication (one-way and two-way) with those involved in the ministry

Partner

Share your responses with another leader. Pray together about what stands out to you from your responses.

Dig Deeper

Read 1 Corinthians 12, 2 Corinthians 3-5, and 1 Peter 5.

PRACTICE

Chapter 11
Plans and Progress

*"If you want to go fast, go alone.
If you want to go far, go together."*
African proverb

*"When you figure out what you
want done, let me know, and I will
get it done."* Church Volunteer

Vision is only good intention
until it is turned into action.
Practically-gifted task people
shine in identifying and carrying
out the details of whom, how,
and when in order to turn vison
into reality.

Every church has its vision printed in the bulletin, hanging
on signs, stamped onto bumper stickers, or placed front and
center on its web site. But is that vision being lived out? For
example, *"To know Christ and make Him known"* is a common
vision statement. Yet the average church rarely sees adults
coming to a newfound faith in Christ.

Imagine a church whose vision emphasized people growing in
Christ-like character. Yet that vision would lose impact if key
leaders of the church were locked in an ongoing conflict with
one another marked by distrust and manipulation. They would
be contradicting the church's vision by their actions.

Living true to our stated vision means aligning how we live and what we do practically. Some people are gifted by nature and experience to focus on the details – what will we do, how much will it cost, how many people will be needed, what materials will be needed, etc. Practically-oriented people focus on tasks to be done. Being at a half-day or full-day vision or strategizing session is like being drilled on by the dentist for them. Yet once vision direction has been decided, the practically-gifted task people shine in identifying and carrying out the details of whom, how, and when, in order to turn vison into reality.

Structure

Some churches have little or no structure. While this may feel exciting as an entrepreneurial and creative environment, an absence of structure can leave a church vulnerable and unstable. Whenever the key-driving personality leaves, a vacuum or crisis is left behind.

The other extreme are churches that have too much structure. The results are people serving a rigid, outdated, or over-sized structure, rather than a structure serving people. Churches with too much structure are like a man who has a coat size of 38 short wearing a 44 long coat. It never fits, and there is always too much empty space. As a rule of thumb, I assume if volunteers serve in more than two roles, then there is too much structure for the size of the church. Like clothing, church structure can and should expand or contract with the size, age, and purpose of the church.

> **If you were starting with a blank canvas,
> what key teams would be vital in order
> to make progress on your vision?**

Teams

If you were starting with a blank canvas, what key teams would be vital in order to make progress on your vision? The goal of teams is not activity or busyness but progress in turning the church's vision into reality. Whether your church calls them teams or committees, those entities should intentionally align with the central purpose of the church. Do you have teams that rarely meet or only maintain a few annual activities? They may need to be redirected or retired.

I have found value in bringing all the teams together periodically in a summit meeting. We share the central vision of the church and the key hoped-for results – dashboard indicators of progress. During the summit, teams can share highlights, questions, and frustrations. Teams are then given "team" time to plan and, if necessary, to partner with other teams in the room. This improves a sense of everyone being part of one movement. If teams meet and plan in isolation, they tend to think only of their specific work. Competing rather than coordinating can result in a form of spiritual Darwinism, as teams compete for money, manpower, and publicity.

Who should lead a team? Whoever is gifted in leading a group. This may or may not be a pastoral staff member. I recommend that board members not lead teams. Instead tap the talent on your team. Having term limits allows fresh faces and perspectives, and prevents control by the same people. Each team should have a staff link with whom they communicate and partner, who also keeps the full staff aware of the team's plans and needs.

Appendix F and G provide several sample worksheets your teams can use for annual goal setting and ongoing information reporting. I ask each team to electronically submit a one-page

"FYI Update" to staff and board members within seven days of each team meeting.

Sometimes a team can struggle with determining practical action steps. When a team feels stuck or uncertain about how to make a key goal become reality, it can be helpful to do a site visit to another ministry that has found an effective way of meeting that same need. I worked with a church that had identified improving its welcome and connection with visitors as a key goal. The Connect Team struggled to develop action steps to accomplish that goal. Team members visited another church in the city with an effective ministry to newcomers. They returned from that site visit enthused, and decided to copy what the other church was doing to welcome newcomers. It was highly successful.

If a team proposes new action that receives mixed reactions, why not put that action on a "trial run" for a year? This calms fears of change while allowing the new action to be tried.

Not every activity will be successful. Encourage and expect teams to annually evaluate the effectiveness of their ministry programs as those programs relate to the core direction and key agreed-upon goals of the church. If a ministry program needs to improve, the team and staff should determine what is needed to make it more effective. If a program is no longer effective or is draining too many resources, lovingly appreciate its history while you retire it. Ending programs can be an emotional battleground. People are better able to accept the end of a favorite program if there has been open communication (why it is being eliminated) and if a replacement is offered (what we will do instead). Eliminating a program and simply leaving a vacuum will frustrate and anger people.

Stories

People believe what we highlight and talk about and what they see modeled in the lives of the leaders. What stories are being shared in your church? What receives emphasis in your verbal, electronic, and written communication? What you talk about is what people assume is important to your church. If your main communication is about recruiting manpower, or about financial needs, then people will assume that subject is what matters most for your church. If you lift up stories of people's lives being changed – newfound faith in Christ, tangible life change in Christ, or the growth from serving – then the congregation will come to believe that your church is about seeing people's lives changed in Christ.

Reflect and Act

1. *What stories have been highlighted in your ministry over the last 6 months?*

   - *What gets talked about most?*

   - *What stories can you share that highlight and reinforce the core direction?*

2. *Is structure too thin or too bloated?*

   - *What changes to structure should you consider?*

   - *Do you have teams? Are they aligned well with the vision? Do we need to adjust teams to align them with the vision?*

   - *How do teams communicate and collaborate with one another and with leadership?*

3. *How are you tapping the talents of the practical task-oriented people? What further steps could be taken to involve those gifted in details, organizing, and practical planning?*

Partner

Share your responses with another leader. Pray together about what stands out to you from your responses.

Dig Deeper

Read 1 Corinthians 12

PRACTICE

Chapter 12
Alignment

My father moved into assisted living several years ago. His home in southern California is now vacant. Slowly we are boxing up dishes, sorting family photos, and selling furniture and household items. When I travel to the West Coast, I stay there. It is starting to feel like a house rather than feeling like "home." Home was where we lived and had our shared memories. Now, in its semi-empty, silent condition, it is reverting to being just a structure, a residence, a "house." Someone else will soon buy it and transform it from a house back into a "home." It struck me that family – shared life with others – is what makes a place "home." The relationships, not the residence, are what change a house into a home.

The same applies to God's family. Our relationships are what make church a family, not the structure we gather in – a church building. The church is called to purposeful relationship, not simply to relationship as an end by itself. As the apostle Paul urged, "*Whatever happens, conduct yourselves in a manner worthy of the gospel of Christ. Then, whether I come and see you or only hear about you in my absence, I will know that you stand firm in the one Spirit, striving together as one for the faith of the gospel.*" Later, in that same letter, he said, "*Make my joy complete by being like-minded, having the same love, being one in spirit and of one mind…. In your relationships with one another, have the same mindset as Christ Jesus.*" (Philippians 1:27, 2:2, 5) As followers of Christ, church is "home" where we practice and grow in living out His purpose in our relationships so we can be Christ-like in the world.

This book is about experiencing the fingerprints of God upon your life and ministry. God's heartbeat is for relationship – moving people God-ward in genuine transformation. The apostle Paul labored until *"Christ is formed in you."* (Galatians 4:19) He was committed to presenting every person *"complete in Christ."* (Colossians 1:28-29) He understood that God intends to morph us (the meaning of transformation) into the image of God (2 Corinthians 3:18).

Alignment gets everything moving in the same direction. If a car is out of alignment, the steering wheel may be centered, but the front tires may veer to the right or to the left. In the same way, alignment in a church moves the entire church body forward in the same direction. Appendix H provides a sample of how one church aligns its structure and roles around its core vision.

How well is your church aligned with the Lord's desires? What aspects of alignment need attention?

Purpose – our single unchanging purpose – is to move people God-ward. God's heart of *splachna* compassion is to become how we treat others – seeing people who are not-yet-believers coming into a living relationship of faith in Christ, and seeing believers growing up in their relationship with Christ. Relationships with others are where we learn to treat others as Christ has treated us – the Vertical becoming the Horizontal. Who is within arm's reach of you (or across the street) that needs the compassion and message of Jesus through your caring? How are you and the church you serve intentionally growing people who live with Christ-like compassion?

Personalities are the wild card and the cause of most church breakdowns. Are you leaning into rather than avoiding or criticizing those different from you? Do you resolve conflicts in God-pleasing rather than Spirit-grieving ways? How are you utilizing different talent on teams to move ministry forward in your church?

Power to move people comes from the Spirit. We are responsible but not powerful enough to move anyone. Pray more, push less. Trust more. Are you a sailboat or a rowboat Christian? How are you cooperating with the pain and brokenness the Lord has allowed in your own life and in the life of your church, in order for Him to prune away self and bring more Christ-like fruit?

Practice – being the leaders God calls us to be – requires roles that clarify how leadership oversees the health and progress of the ministry. How is the health of the working relationship between the board and the pastor? Are roles clear and lived out well? Does your structure fit your size and needs? How are you using teams to engage and maximize the talent within the body?

While fictional, I am moved by the story imagining the resurrected Jesus returning to enter heaven. Eager angels crowd around Him to hear Jesus share about His earthly ministry. He describes His three years of public ministry, the miracles, the crowds, and His suffering and death. The angels ask what happens now. Jesus replies, "*I have placed twelve men in charge of spreading the gospel and making disciples worldwide.*" Stunned, the angels express their concern. "*But these few men are not the brightest. Some already have denied knowing You. If they fail, what is Plan B?*" Jesus says, "*There is no Plan B.*"

Indeed, there is no "Plan B." God calls Christians into a restored and vibrant vertical relationship with Himself, and to loving and caring horizontal relationships with believers and not-yet believers.

Our calling is worth it. The world for which Jesus gave His life needs the body of Christ to be who it is, because if it is who it ain't, then it ain't who it is.

APPENDICES

The appendices that follow are samples and worksheets for your own use. Digital versions are available at info@progressandjoy.net

Appendix A
Sample Biblical Passages –
Purpose of Leadership

[The Scriptures below can be used for personal study or as a group discussion.]

What are you seeing about God's heart? What does He care MOST about?

OLD TESTAMENT samples:

Genesis 12:1-3	Exodus 6:6-7	Exodus 19:4-6
Deuteronomy 4:20	Deuteronomy 7:6-14	Deuteronomy 14:2
Psalm 42:1	Psalm 63:1-2	Psalm 67

Each of the prophets (major and minor)

NEW TESTAMENT samples:

Matthew 11:28-30	Matthew 28:18-20	Mark 2:16-17
Luke 15:20-24	John 3:16	John 10:10
John 13:34-35	John 14:6	John 15:1, 8-11
John 17:21-24	Romans 5:6-11	Romans 8:31-39
Romans 12:1-2	1 Corinthians 13	2 Corinthians 3:18
2 Corinthians 5:17-21	Galatians 4:19	Galatians 5:6, 13, 22-23
Ephesians 1:18-22	Ephesians 2:17-22	Ephesians 3:16-20
Ephesians 4:1-24	Philippians 1:25	Philippians 3:7-15

Colossians 1:13-15, 28	1 Thessalonians 1:7-10	1 Timothy 1:5
Hebrews 12:10	James 4:4-5	1-2 John
1 Peter 2:9-10	Revelation 5:9-10	Revelation 21:3-4

APPENDIX B
Small Group Leader Feedback

This feedback form can be used by pastors and trainers with existing small group leaders to coach them on leading effective small groups. It works best as a follow-up to an in-person site visit observing the group in action.

Group_____

Date of site visit_____

Site visitor _____

Caring: Giving and receiving support

1. *Circle which words describe how people feel?*
   Welcomed   safe   included
            cared about   alone   ignored

2. *Circle how newcomers and absentees feel:*
   Welcomed   safe   included
            cared about   alone   ignored

3. *Check which aspects of caring were practiced well:*
   ____Warm welcome and refreshments
   ____Attentive listening
   ____Personal encouragement
   ____Sharing experiences, offering wisdom to one another
   ____Prayer with and for one another
   ____Action to meet practical needs
   ____Other

Growing: Movement in lives from God's truth and from sharing together

Check which of these took place during the group time:

____Truth from God's word that had practical/personal application
____Engagement of most or all group members sharing comments)
____Lecture or a few dominating the conversation
____Stories of growth shared by others in the group
____Utilizing/developing the talents in our group

Serving: Outreach to not-yet-believers woven into the regular rhythm of the group

Check which of these took place during the group time:

____Names of not-yet-believers were: _____
_____
____Shared and prayed for
____Caring action steps were taken (what we will do to reach out in love)
____Readiness to birth a new group

APPENDIX C
Responding to Conflict

[This is a one-page summary of chapter 8 on resolving conflict.]

<u>Spirit-grieving and God-pleasing responses to relational conflict</u>

<u>Spirit-grieving reactions in conflict:</u>
Fighting and blaming – Galatians 5:15

False peace – Proverbs 26:23-26, 28

Gossip – Proverbs 6:16-19, Proverbs 16:28

<u>God-pleasing responses in conflict</u>
Don't get started – Proverbs 17:14, Romans 14:1

Self-examination – Matthew 7:5

Keep the circle as small as possible – Matthew 18:15, James 1:19-20

Get "helpful help" – Matthew 18:16, Philippians 4:2

Live at peace, as much as it depends on you – Romans 12:18

Grow from the pain – Matthew 18:21-35, John 15:1-12, Ephesians 4:29-5:2, Hebrews 12;1-15

APPENDIX D
Table of Contents of Elder Manual

Board Manual Sections
(From Ecclesia – a church in Hollywood, California)

Mission
- Mission Statement
- Dashboard Outcomes
- Lead Team Key Objectives

Ministry Flow
- Lead Teams Circle Graphic
- Discipleship: 5 stages of Spiritual Formation
- Missiology
- Current Outreach Partners

Elder Board [1]
- Elder Board Culture
- Elder and Pastor Roles
- Elder Expectations
- Big Rocks

Policies

History

Doctrine and Theology
- Statement of Faith
- Doctrinal Distinctives and Guidelines

---

[1] Author Note: The items included under "Elder Board" are set forth in greater detail on the next two pages.

Other

- List of Staff Names & Positions
- List of Elders
- Officers of the corporation
- Conflict of Interest Policy

Elder Board

Elder Board Culture

Elders will consciously live and model team and healthy relationships, meaning we aim for the elder board to be characterized by:

1. Spirit Dependence — prayer individually and together; listening to the Lord and to one another; leading in faith; courage to follow His will and doing it in His way
2. Grace and Truth — honesty with one another blended with accepting, bearing with, and forgiving one another in love, including healthy resolution of conflicts
3. Servant Leaders — seek activation of the body (Ephesians 4:12-16) and live out a collaborative culture (within the elders, as well as elder-staff and empowering lead teams and the body) and eschewing a top down "control" approach to leadership
4. Realistic Demands — efficient use of elder time, including: productive meetings, actionable assignments, accountability, and follow through
5. Group Authority vs. Individual authority

Elder and Pastor Roles

Pastors are also biblical elders, but they have a unique and distinct, different role from lay elders.

1. Elders — Responsible for shepherding the church through care, prayer, and discipline; leading and overseeing mission, policies, Big Rocks, doctrine, lead pastor's annual evaluation, hiring and firing of pastors, financial decisions, legal and fiduciary responsibilities of the nonprofit organization;

attending bimonthly meetings (2-3 hours each), with one meeting focused on shepherding, and the second focused on leading and administration; attending additional meetings (with ministry staff) and retreat/training sessions.

2. Lead Pastor – Responsible for managing and developing staff; hiring and firing staff; establishing healthy working relationship with pastors and ministry lead staff; ex-officio member (non-voting) of elder board; present at all elder meetings.

3. Pastors – Elders in the biblical (spiritual role) sense; not part of elder meetings except when invited based on matters in their ministry area or when Lead Pastor with Elder chair deems appropriate; hiring/firing of pastors is an elder responsibility.

4. Elder Emeriti – Utilize the experience and perspective past elders possess by activating them when appropriate (task teams, advisory roles, guest presence at certain meetings, etc.).

Elder Expectations

Elder Meeting Norms and Expectations

1. Bimonthly Meetings
   - I Shepherding meeting (2-3 hours)
   - I Administration meeting (2-3 hours)
2. Periodic Elder and Staff combined meeting
3. Elder Retreats and Training Sessions
4. Town Hall Meetings (church-wide informational meetings)
5. Shepherding
   - Care, discipline
   - Presence and participation in church life/programs
6. Plan and/or lead special services as agreed upon

Big Rocks

Big rocks are key items elders are responsible for. Elders may delegate due diligence to existing or specially created ad hoc teams, but the final decision for Big Rock items rests with the Elder Board.

Elders are urged to delegate any items that another person or group is capable of handling.

<u>Big Rocks</u>
1. Doctrinal Positions
   - Including determination of communication and adherence
2. Policies
3. Financial Integrity and Sound Stewardship
4. Continuity of Elder culture and roles as terms turn over
   - Including nomination process, elder orientation, training
5. Mission and Dashboard Outcomes
6. Annual Performance Evaluation of Lead Pastor
7. Hiring and Firing of Pastoral Staff
8. Staff Ratios
9. Communication with Staff and Community
10. Discipline
    - Including conflict resolution within the body

APPENDIX E
Church Check-Up Sample

(From a major multi-site church near St. Paul, Minnesota)

Our church is at a FORK IN THE ROAD....

OPPORTUNITY
-*"make the most of every opportunity"* (Ephesians 5:13-17)
- we are a mature church that recognizes its needs and is "ready"
- act on the clarity and fresh conviction found in the Check-Up
- a 'holy shift' from maintenance to missional...
'transformational followers'

RISK
- 'missing' this opportunity, not taking the fork in the road
- urgency...a crisis is looming if we do not act
- doing it ourselves apart from the Spirit as the change agent

---

Deut. 1 – *spies into the land...go by faith or shrink back in fear?...consequences of each,*
Acts 11 – *Peter's uncomfortable, transforming experience*

Commit to *a new scorecard* that measures progress in several key areas:

FELLOWSHIP (the great commandment "love one another") - easy, clear ways to feel 'welcomed' and 'connected' are needed that include inter-generational connections/mentoring. There is a feeling of 'insiders' and 'outsiders'. This is about relational 'connections', feeling a sense of belonging. Connecting people, small groups, discipleship/mentoring all need improvement. More than just a social activity, the data points to Fellowship improving "outreach" by becoming more 'others-oriented'.

Adults and Youth all rate this a high priority. Fellowship received the most number of Dream Clouds.

COMPASSION/OUTREACH, EVANGELISM (the great commission "go and make disciples of all nations") – needs to become a 'way of life', part of our DNA. There is a recognition and readiness for a change of heart. Data findings pointed to the need for equipping and concrete opportunities, as well as hearing stories of results. Can we take our strength in Missions and tap and deploy it locally?

SERVANT LEADERS – systems and equipping/mentoring of servant leaders are needed so that we are developing and mobilizing talent, rather than relying on the same pool of volunteers. This extends beyond "serving" in church, and includes equipping people for outreach to our community. Consensus and Dream comments talk about: need for training and a discipleship "process"; desire for mentoring (19 red dot statements). Servant Leaders received twice as many red as green dots. Our second campus has had staff turnover and is looking for leadership training and direction from staff.

The above three priorities need to be both "top down" (staff and leadership driving them) as well as "bottom up" (embraced and engaged in by all of us). In other words – everyone needs to 'buy-in' and leadership needs to lead this thrust.

Recommendations

1. Follow Christ's unique calling to become "better not bigger". Agree to a **new scorecard** that places priority on *Outreach* (to those who do not yet know Christ), *Fellowship* (welcoming and connecting; common bond as 1 church); and *Servant Leaders* (training, mentoring to develop people in whom love for others, including not-yet-Christians is a 'way of life.'

2. "Embed" **equipping/mentoring** into our current adult programs (Sunday adult Bible fellowship classes and small groups, etc.) as a key means of changing our DNA and growing us in outreach as a 'way of life.'

3. Identify the **demographic realities and needs in our surrounding community.** Which are being well-served by other churches? Which do our people have a heart for serving?

4. **Fellowship**: determine easy, known ways of connecting people so they feel 'part of' rather than an outsider. Questions to consider: what is working in other churches re: assimilating newcomers? Is hospitality a means of inter-generational connecting? Do Sunday adult Bible fellowship classes limit inter-generational opportunities? Review and identify ways to improve small groups and mentoring.

5. **Develop servant leaders** – commit to a "system" that identifies, develops, and utilizes lay leaders.

6. **Prayer** – Devote time to a season of Prayer in repentance, and renewed love and commitment being "one" body of Christ, with a renewed heart and will for reaching our world.

7. **Communication** – The new Communications ministry should develop ways to consistently and effectively communicate opportunities and resulting stories of impact in lives.

Implications for Senior Pastor Search

- dream comments focused on new senior pastor being a great biblical preacher with application; leader/direction, unifying campuses
- our need to change our DNA to a heart for and effectiveness in outreach suggest a new pastor needs to personally

have a lifestyle of interacting with not-yet-Christians and a track record of turning a church more to an outward, missional focus

- our fellowship need paints a picture of a pastor who enjoys people...who is a people-person
- leadership (both staff and lay) development would indicate that we need an experienced, "equipper/mentor" who finds satisfaction from equipping and others to 'do ministry'
- Our grace-based evangelicalism suggests a need for a pastor who aligns with this, not just theologically but in how he pastorally does relationships

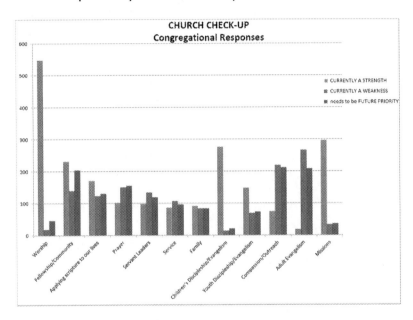

APPENDIX F
FYI Report Form

FYI Report from _____ for month of _____
from staff and ministry teams to elders and staff

The purpose of the FYI reports is to update leadership about what is going on in your area of ministry. FYI Reports should be one-half to one page in length. Send FYI Report electronically to your contact at least 7 days prior to the upcoming board meeting.

(1) Currently we are working on...

(2) Here is what we have planned in the next 3 months:

(3) Good things we want you to be aware of are... a 'story' to share...

(4) Needs, frustrations, and problems in our area we want you to be aware of are...

(5) "We are thinking about" -- dreams, ideas, possibilities

(6) Our prayer requests [list from 2-4 most important items for prayer]

Items to be considered to go onto Board meeting agenda
Discussion Items [estimate of time required]

Decision Items [discussed at previous board meeting - now ready for board decision]

APPENDIX G
Lead Team Worksheet

[Type your ministry's core vision statement here]

1. **Goals:** How will our team significantly contribute to the vision?

    - What are the 2-3 goals we will focus on carrying out this year?

    - What will we need to make each goal a reality?

    - What do we need to know/find out/research/explore?

    - Calendar: By when we will act on our plans?

2. **Resources:** What will be needed for us to be successful?

    - Manpower – Who will do it?

    - Materials – Money, training, publicity, etc.

3. **Coordination:** Who else [teams or people] will you team up with to make it happen?

4. **Communication**: Who needs to know, and how will you inform them? (Staff, elders, community, other team leads?)

5. **Care:** How will your team minister to those on your team?

6. **Follow-Through:**

    - Who will send out written agendas in advance?
    - Who will send out brief, clear minutes within 5 days after each Lead Team meeting?
    - Do you need to add more people to your team? What type of skills/experience are needed? What will you do?

- How will you keep your eyes on your 2-3 key goals throughout the year?
- How will you share progress we as a church can all celebrate?

Team _____ Chair _____

Staff link _____
Date submitted to leadership _____

APPENDIX H
Aligning Vision with Roles and Structure Sample

The sample below is a visual illustrating how one church organizes and programs to stay aligned with the vision. Brief written descriptions of roles are listed on the following page titled Ministry Flow - Roles.

Use this sample to check alignment. Your staff and team names may differ, but is there alignment so that every aspect of the church life is linked (no orphan programs) and all are serving to further the vision?

Appendix H
Ministry Flow Sample
"Oversight" by Lead Pastor and Governing Board

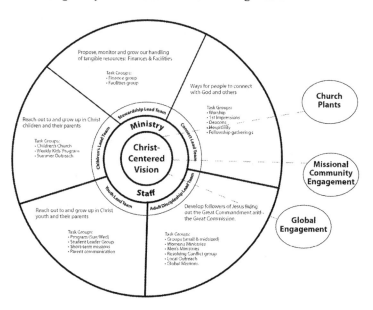

"Developing followers of Jesus who live as salt and light in the world."

Ministry Flow - Roles
(1 Cor 12 – How Ministry Happens)

Elders – "overseers" responsible for:
- Doctrine
- Direction (strategic vision)
- Healthy collaborative working relationship with lead pastor (leadership, administration)
- Shepherding needs or congregation
- Annual evaluation of lead pastor
- Communication between leadership and congregation
- Tasks specified in by-laws

Lead Pastor – primary responsible person for translating strategic mission into action through staff and volunteers
- Plus tasks specified in by-laws and letter of call

Teams – responsible to <u>decide action steps</u> (and <u>implementation)</u> to accomplish goals that turn strategic vision into reality
- Each team will have a link to formal leadership (staff, elders) for coordination and communication
- All teams are expected to intentionally pull in/align with the strategic vision (i.e. – pet projects, preserving "legacy" programs, guarding turf is frowned upon)
- Teams have the freedom to determine HOW to get it done (program, activities), including freedom to create "table groups"; with staff approval
- KISS – simple, easy to understand structure; few teams rather than too many teams

Printed in the United States
By Bookmasters